APERITIF

A SPIRITED GUIDE TO
THE DRINKS, HISTORY AND
CULTURE OF THE APERITIF

KATE HAWKINGS

quadrille

PHOTOGRAPHY BY SARAH HOGAN

Publishing Director and Editor: Sarah Lavelle
Designer: Will Webb
Photographer: Sarah Hogan
Prop Stylist: Alexander Breeze
Copy Editor: Euan Ferguson
Production: Vincent Smith and Nikolaus Ginelli

First published in 2018 by Quadrille,
an imprint of Hardie Grant Publishing

Quadrille
52–54 Southwark Street
London SE1 1UN
quadrille.com

Cataloguing in Publication Data: a catalogue record for this book
is available from the British Library.

ISBN: 978 1 78713 126 2

Printed in China

CONTENTS

INTRODUCTION

I WAS 12 WHEN I FIRST HEARD THE WORD 'aperitif', at a chintzy country house hotel that reeked of uptight gentility and suppressed emotions. I was there to celebrate my great aunt Margaret's eightieth birthday. My parents, my older sister and I were ushered into the drawing room before dinner, Margaret gamely leading the way on her walking sticks, with her ill-fitting wig set at a jaunty angle. We perched on the over-stuffed sofas overloaded with cushions as leather-bound menus were flourished by the white-jacketed maitre d', sleek of hair and oleaginous of demeanour. Our host then uttered the immortal words, 'Would you care to commence with an aperitif?'

My sister issued a snort and my shoulders started shaking, but we managed to summon the good manners to wait until the poor man left the room before collapsing in hysterical giggles at this preposterous pomposity. When my father, who dined here occasionally with his clients, leaned towards us and whispered conspiratorially, 'His name is Mr Snodgrass,' we totally lost the plot, spluttering dry-roasted peanuts across the velvet pile carpet and crossing our legs tightly so we wouldn't wet our pants.

Our mother frowned and handed us the tissues she always carried in her handbag; we wiped the snot from our noses and regained a semblance of composure just as Mr Snodgrass returned with our drinks held aloft on a silver salver. Aunt Margaret said simply, 'Well, isn't this nice?'

It was bitter lemon for my sister and me – the go-to treat drink whenever it was on offer – while the ladies had champagne and my father, a Campari Soda. The drinks arrived in immaculate crystal glassware, a ramrod-stiff linen coaster deftly placed beneath each one by the fawning Mr S. He produced his pen and notebook with a flourish. 'And may I take your order for dinner?' At that moment a passion in my heart was born for the aperitif – the very word, the sense of occasion, and my-oh-my, the drinks.

Campari Soda is my absolute favourite aperitif; from time to time I replace the soda with bitter lemon and drink in homage to dear Mr Snodgrass.

The word 'aperitif' comes from the Latin *aperire*, meaning 'to open'. It is something to open the appetite, to stimulate the taste buds, to mark the start of a meal that's to come. It could be a perfect gin and tonic before a long and louche lunch that ends the wrong side of midnight, a Martini to flex the digestive muscles at the start of a dinner out with friends, or perhaps a glass of something lovely at a bar on your way home for supper.

More usually for most of us, an aperitif is what properly announces the opening of the evening at home at the end of a long day when we turn our attention to the important things in life – perhaps cooking, eating, drinking and talking with the one or ones we love, or just slugging something into a glass, making cheese on toast and snuggling up solo with friends on social media. Some cocktails can be considered aperitifs, and champagne certainly counts; a glass of wine can't put a foot wrong if it has a crispy pizazz to get your juices flowing and a snifter of sherry will always suit, but *apéros*, as the French fondly call them, can be so much more.

Many of the classic aperitifs date back centuries and have their roots in medicinal compounds that all manner of chemists, alchemists, quacks and clergy concocted using whatever nearby nature offered. Such drinks were usually devised to aid digestion; water was often contaminated and food hygiene standards were slack, so the digestive health of populations needed all the help it could get. Where there's medicine, there's money, particularly if the tincture tasted good, so making snifters to be taken before eating became big business.

The histories of many of these drinks are lost in the mists and alcoholic daze of yore; others are newer to the aperitif party, the result of the vogue in the drinking business to resurrect and revive forgotten recipes as well as to use them as inspiration for new drinks for the modern age.

Aperitifs occupy a particular niche in drinking land. Cocktails are all well and good in the drinker's repertoire, but the aperitif suggests something rather lighter, something to tickle one's fancy without wrestling one's taste buds and sobriety into submission. There is a trend towards drinking lighter alcohol and less of it, and the aperitif vibe fits this bill perfectly. Also, they don't need the hand of a skilled bartender so are easy to knock up at home.

Sharpeners, snifters, aperitivos or noggins (my granny's word, and perhaps my favourite): we all know what we mean. Let us raise a glass to the aperitif, that most civilised and cheering of drinking habits.

1
THE STORY OF THE APERITIF

THE DRINKING OF APERITIFS is an indisputably European thing. Across the continent there endures a culture of finishing the day with a stroll in the sun and a drink in a bar, seeing and being seen on leafy boulevards in towns and cities or promenades on the coast, or perhaps just a very slow amble around the village square. The Spanish call this daily ritual *el paseo*; the Italians, *la passeggiata*. In Britain we call it 'going down the pub'.

We Brits lack the balmy weather enjoyed across the Channel – one is far more likely to make a dash in the rain to one's local than enjoy a leisurely saunter underneath the beating sun – but whereas most of us used to be happy with warm ale or white wine when we got there, we now crave more fitting and interesting things. Traditional boozers are closing at an astonishing rate: the more canny owners and brands have transformed themselves into modern bars for the modern drinker, offering cocktails, craft beers and wines that go far beyond just 'red or white'.

The precise history of drinking cultures and what they drank is shrouded in mystery, myth and muddled memories after one too many. Research sends one down endless rabbit-holes of information, much of it fascinating, much contradictory. In researching this book I have driven myself to drink on several occasions at the impossibility of establishing the facts. Of one thing we can be sure: mankind has been drinking alcohol for a very long time indeed.

Alcohol is produced by the action of yeasts on anything that contains sugars, the yeast feeding on the sugar to produce carbon dioxide and alcohol. Back in the days when our distant ancestors were still swinging from the trees, fruits would drop to the forest floor as they ripened to full sweetness – natural yeasts borne in the air would feed on the sugars within, starting the process of fermentation. The smell of alcohol made the fruit easier to find than when it was growing on the plant; in addition, animals would have experienced a gentle rush of pleasure as the alcohol released feel-good serotonin, dopamine and endorphins into their brains.

At this point I will posit the controversial and possibly gin-fuelled theory that this extra appeal to life on the ground tempted apes down from the trees, and thus alcohol is indirectly responsible for the evolution of all human life. Though, squiffy primates would have been easy for other animals to hunt – so perhaps it was the ones who could take their booze that survived, rather than the fittest. Around 10 million years ago, a gene mutation in the last common ancestor shared between us and the apes created an enzyme that digested alcohol 40 times faster. This allowed the fruits of the forest floor and the nutrition they gave to be enjoyed in greater quantity without being so susceptible to the ill effects.

The following chasm of time remains somewhat woolly. The first archaeological evidence of concerted production of grain-based hooch was found in Turkey, at what's thought to be a temple site nearly 10,000 years old, where trough-shaped stone vessels with a capacity of around 40 gallons bear traces of a fermented broth. It was only a couple of millennia afterwards that grapes were being cultivated to ferment into wine in modern-day Iran, Georgia and Armenia.

We do know that the Romans drank wine infused with medicinal herbs said to aid digestion at the start of their elaborate and excessive feasts, and of course we have their language to thank for the word *aperitif* itself.

The Dark Ages are known as such for good reason – there is precious little in the way of written records for the centuries following the decline of the Roman Empire (although we can be certain that the production of alcohol predates the written word). Wine continued to be made and drunk in those places where the climate suited the growing of grapes, and we know mead, made by fermenting honey in water, was all the rage in the chillier Celtic and Germanic cultures. Beer from grains and cider from apples were also made at this time, though how they'd compare with today's brews is, frankly, anyone's guess.

Meanwhile, alchemists in the Arab world in the 10th (or was it the 8th?) century were working on the art of distillation, a process that may (or may not) have been practised by the Greeks or even the Babylonians before them. Or was it the Egyptians? Whatever. In their quest to find the true 'spirit' of a substance these Arabic distillers boiled it and condensed the vapours produced in a device called an alembic still. This process was used to make perfumes, medicines and cosmetics, including a fine dark powder used by ladies to enhance their eyes. *Al-kohl*; the probable root of our word *alcohol*.

When wines or other fermented brews were distilled they produced a high-strength alcohol known as 'spirited water' or 'water of life', from which we get the generic word 'spirit' for any distilled alcohol, and the specific drinks *eau de vie* in France and *akvavit* in Scandinavia, and (possibly) whisky (*uisce beatha* in Gaelic), which all mean 'water of life'.

These distilling techniques found their way to Europe, possibly to Salerno in southern Italy in the 12th century, or Bologna in the 13th. Some time around 1320, Pierre-Arnaud de Villeneuve, a physician living in Montpellier in France, wrote his *Liber de Vinum* (Book of Wine) in which he describes the distillation of wine to make a spirit.

De Villeneuve discovered that when a little of this spirit was added to wine it not only halted fermentation, so leaving residual sugars and thus natural sweetness, it also prevented the wine from oxidising and turning into vinegar. This process is called fortification and it became central to the development of so many aperitifs that we know today.

While we have religion to blame for many of the world's evils, we also have it to thank for its influence on the worlds of both medicine and merriment over the following centuries. Christians needed sacramental wine so most religious orders made their own, as well as other remedial drinks and medicines made from distillations of plants found in their surrounding lands. Those that were situated on trade routes would have discovered new spices and ingredients from the passing merchants who sought refuge with them – most monasteries offered accommodation for pilgrims and other travellers along what must have been long and solitary paths. We should give a special mention to the Benedictine order of monks and nuns in particular, whose research into herbal cures and other tinctures, as well as a probable love of a tipple to take the edge off those dark and lonely nights of the soul, features so much in the history of many of the alcoholic drinks that we still enjoy.

La Belle Epoque, that period of relative peace, prosperity and a flourishing of technology and the arts that swept across Europe between the end of the Franco-Prussian war in 1871 and the start of World War I in 1914, was good news for the aperitif. In towns and cities across Europe, wide streets and boulevards were built, perfect for promenading, and where there used to be lowly cafés and bars rose large and lavish establishments to cater for the newly rich and leisured. Walls of mirrors and finely carved woodwork stood by gleaming brass rails and hissing gas lights, all swathed in a fug of smoke: in these pleasure-domes the genteel appeal of the aperitif was democratised, at least up to a point.

This was the age of the flâneur, the preening peacock dressed to the nines, out on the town to see and be seen in all the right places, drinking all the right things. The power of branding had dawned on forward-thinking producers – Henri-Louis Pernod was one of the first off the mark, his modish advertising for absinthe being widely credited with spreading the drink's popularity like wildfire, and other producers soon followed suit. Brands became associated with status and were targeted directly at the growing middle classes with great effect. This was the age of the train as well as of rampant commerce, so what had been only local drinks for local people became what we'd now call global brands.

The Americans had been drinking cocktails since the early 1800s, aided and abetted by the introduction of refrigeration and commercially produced ice, but this modern cocktail culture didn't reach Europe until 'American bars' began to open in grand hotels in the late 19th century. New Yorker Jerry Thomas, gold prospector, showman and all-round bon viveur, carved himself a niche as the bartender's bartender with his seminal 1862 book *How to Mix Drinks* (or *The Bon Vivant's Companion*). Thomas combined craftsmanship with showmanship and his flamboyant style earned him celebrity status wherever he went. He travelled widely throughout the United States and Europe and spread the seeds of his new cocktail style, coining the term 'mixologist'.

After post-war gloom had lifted and the television age dawned, stars of stage and screen were rolled out to endorse all the accoutrements of middle class aspiration. Pre-dinner drinks were very much a part of this. Those less junior than some will fondly remember **Cinzano** being peddled by a glamorous Joan Collins and hapless Leonard Rossiter, while Humphrey Bogart and, er, Lorraine Chase flirted with each other over **Campari** in a pastiche of *Casablanca*. And who could forget Orson Welles' gravelly tones extolling the pleasure of **Domecq's La Ina** sherry?

These were the days when 'Happiness is a cigar called Hamlet', when **Martini & Rosso**'s vermouths were being pushed against backdrops of beautiful people skiing, sailing and hot-air ballooning, a glass of Martini with ice rarely out of shot, with the strapline 'Any time, any place, anywhere'. These ads had a knowing kind of wit along with a message that sophistication was only a slice of lemon away. And, of course, the right brand mattered. The marketing of drink brands really ramped up in the 1970s and '80s, promising to confer on us glamour and status along with squiffiness.

Then came the Cocktail Years, given a boost by the execrable 1988 film *Cocktail*, in which Tom Cruise introduced us to 'flair bartending' – the ridiculous show-off circus trickery of juggling bottles, shakers and other bar tools RATHER THAN JUST GETTING ON AND MAKING THE BLOODY DRINK. To be fair, Jerry Thomas was known for such theatrics in the 19th century, but that doesn't make it right. Some things never change: good bars are and always have been those where the guests are treated as guests and not as audiences to fawn at the feet of their performing hosts. It is no surprise that the quality of drinks in those days was pretty dire.

Sugary cocktails adorned with novelty straws and gaudy non-ironic umbrellas were the order of the day. This was the heyday of the Piña Colada, the Blue Lagoon and the Slippery Nipple; of bartenders in Hawaiian shirts surrounded by plastic palm trees. Wham's 1983 song 'Club Tropicana' and its accompanying video just about sum it up.

As the uncool eighties gave way to the narcissistic nineties, sensible bartenders with better taste and style looked to Jerry Thomas's *How to Mix Drinks*, as well as Harry Craddock's 1930 *Savoy Cocktail Book* and others, for inspiration. This trend started in America and spread to cool bars in Germany; London was a little late to the party but when it arrived it made a lot of noise. Cosmopolitans and Whiskey Sours, Moscow Mules and Mai Tais,

Caipirinhas and their Cuban cousins Mojitos, served by sexy barmen (and yes, they were, and still are, mostly men) with naughty twinkles in their eyes. There was a sense of elegant debauchery to these proceedings held in new-age, glamorous bars, as well as real geekery – top bartenders became minor celebrities who revived and refined the classics and brought us new drinks to be taken seriously, made with an eagle eye for detail and an obsessive tongue for quality.

Drinks that were strong and bitter became the fashion; Negronis took centre stage again after decades in the doldrums, and vermouths and other traditional aperitifs also came blinking into the light once more, with fashionable bars experimenting with their own concoctions, infusing spirits with botanicals to make their own house versions.

Cocktails have been on a roll since then, as aperitifs and digestifs as well as insalubrious nights of getting hammered with nothing but a bowl of nuts for sustenance. But cocktails are damaging on the pocket and on one's liver; we now see a trend towards lighter drinking and this is where aperitifs really come into their own.

THE APERITIF ACROSS EUROPE

We should doff our caps to the **ITALIANS,** who can lay claim to have come up with the aperitif concept in the first place, dating as far back as the Romans. Aperitivo-time in the royal courts of the 18th century involved taking a glass of the new-fangled **vermouth** with a morsel of food before yet another lavish dinner began. The habit was embraced by all walks of life and is still alive and well across the country, engrained into the daily ritual of life, from *alla moda* bars in Milan's grand piazzas to grubby shacks down backstreets in Naples.

In Venice *Andémo béver un'ombra!* is shorthand for 'let's go for a drink', though the literal translation of *ombra* is 'shadow'. This refers to the practice going back centuries when wine would be sold from mobile carts that were moved as the day went on so they were always in the shadow of the campanile – the bell tower – of the San Marco cathedral, the better to keep the wine cool. Nowadays the **Aperol Spritz** is Venice's best-selling aperitif, with **Bellinis** – said to be invented in Harry's Bar on the San Marco waterfront – surely not far behind. The Milanese prefer **Campari,** it being invented there, while vermouths are often the order of the day for the good citizens of Turin. **White wine,** sparkling or otherwise, with or without the addition of an additional flavouring, is popular across the country too and, of course, all Italians love a **Negroni.**

Wherever you are and whatever you're drinking, an *aperitivo* in Italy is unthinkable without some food. This civilised practice allows for leisurely drinking without getting silly on alcohol fed to an empty stomach. Bread, cheese, cured meats, olives, perhaps some deep-fried *suppli* (rice balls) or some anchovies fresh from the sea; salty things to titillate the taste buds and keep a relatively clear head before dinner.

In **SPAIN** the **G&T** is king; the Spanish are the world's third largest **gin** consumers (the Filipinos drink the most, then the Americans; the Brits are fourth in the gin lovers' hit parade) but they tend to drink it as a post-prandial rather than to mark the end of the day. When it comes to aperitifs, different regions have different habits, although a *caña* of cold **beer** to kick off an evening is ubiquitous across the country. **Sherry,** of course, in Andalusia, while the hipsters of Barcelona and hip-in-their-own-way Galicians prefer **vermouth** (*vermut*, as they call it there). In the north, the Asturians and the Basques drink their local **cider,** poured from a height to give it some fizz, or their young white wine served in a similar fashion. Always, always preprandials in Spain are knocked back with something to eat – nuts or a nibble of ham or cheese, or perhaps a nugget of tortilla. These are true tapas – from *tapa,* meaning 'a cover', as these morsels of food were originally served on small saucers placed on the top of the glass to keep the flies off.

The **FRENCH** are still traditionalists when it comes to their *apéros* – they've never been big on vodka or gin but prefer **pastis, sparkling wine** (rarely still wine unless it's made into a **kir**), and when it comes to vermouths they tend to stick to the big brands, the **Martinis** and the **Cinzanos** as well as their own **Noilly Prat, Dubonnet** and the splendid **Dolin** range of vermouths from Chambéry. They're also some of the world's keenest **port** consumers, generally preferring chilled red port of fair-to-middling quality as an aperitif to the more serious vintage and tawny wines we Brits, still stuck in our own traditional ways when it comes to port, have with cheese and often only at Christmas.

2
THE PERFECT
APPETISER

APERITIFS ARE MORE THAN just an aesthetic or psychological stimulant of the appetite; there is solid science that shows they set the body up for the food in a physiological fashion and they do this in various ways.

Many alcoholic drinks have evolved from herbal medicines made from plants that were, rightly or wrongly, thought to aid digestion and/or cure so many gastric complaints. Wormwood, gentian and cinchona crop up in so many of them, along with countless other leaves, roots, fruits and barks that were macerated, extracted, fermented and/or distilled. A characteristic of most of these is their bitter taste.

Bitterness is a taste that crops up in many aperitifs; it is also an indicator of poison. If we ingest poison our bodies are wired to get rid of it as quickly as possible so, in response to the sensation of bitterness, warning signs from the brain tell the digestive system to ramp up into action. A complex series of physiological responses kick in: as well as making us salivate, bitterness triggers the release of endorphins to speed digestion and adrenaline to break down toxins in our stomach. These are warnings of possible danger ahead – they also raise our heart rate and make us feel heady and pleasantly high, which is probably why humans are the biggest risk-takers in the animal kingdom. We flirt with danger because it gives us a frisson of pleasure; we like bitterness in drinks because it smacks of menace.

But it is not only bitterness that makes a drink an effective aperitif. Alcohol itself clears the palate by rinsing molecules lingering in the pores on the surface of our tongues – it is particularly effective at dissolving stubborn non-water-soluble fats – thus encouraging digestion-aiding salivation.

Neat vodka is probably the most effective palate cleanser though hardly the most pleasant to drink, which is where a fizzy mixer comes in. The tingling sensation of the bubbles on your tongue also encourages salivation as well as a sense of cleansing, and the smaller the bubbles the more effective this is.

Carbon dioxide – the gas that makes bubbles – is more soluble in alcohol than it is in water, so the bubbles are smaller than in soft drinks (champagne and other fizzy wines, take a bow), although the sugar in tonic water and other mixers helps to stabilise the bubbles and so give the required effect.

There is some confusion as to whether fizzy mixers make the alcohol hit the bloodstream faster than if it was drunk neat. While there is some evidence that this is the case, sugar is known to slow absorption so it may well cancel out the effects of the bubbles. This is why sugar-free mixers appear to speed up drunkenness: another good reason, as if the taste wasn't bad enough, not to drink diet tonic water. Sugar releases dopamine, a neurotransmitter associated with reward and pleasure, into our bloodstream, while artificial sweeteners do not. Artificial sweeteners also bond tightly to receptors in our taste buds and leave that distinctively unpleasant metallic aftertaste that's hard to wash away.

Too much sweetness deadens the appetite, as does too much umami, that deeply savoury fifth sense we associate with Marmite, parmesan cheese and soy sauce, which is why a Bloody Mary, with the sweetness of the tomato juice set against the savoury seasonings, so often seems like a meal in itself. We in the restaurant trade used to call Saturday morning Bloody Marys 'electric soup': just enough alcohol to give the required lift and enough sustenance to keep hunger pangs at bay until our post-lunch-service grub. Sometimes we'd have another, just to keep us going.

Astringency and saltiness also make you salivate – fino and manzanilla sherry, for example, or dry white wines, or anything garnished with lemon or lime – so it's no coincidence that much of the food that's so fitting with aperitifs echoes these sentiments too – think roasted nuts, a modest crisp, slivers of salty cheese and/or salami, an olive or even a pickled egg still tangy from its brine.

All our senses are engaged when we drink. We use our sight to assess the initial demeanour of what's in store – is it pretty and pale, perhaps with bubbles, or is it something tantalisingly dark and brooding? Is it served straight up, glorious in its nakedness, or does it come over ice with a compelling garnish? Does it look like something we'd like to drink?

Our sense of smell gives us more of a clue as we raise the glass to our lips; we always get the aromas – what those in the booze biz call the 'nose', never the 'bouquet' – before we get the taste. Fruity, floral, grassy, herbaceous, with notes of spice, nuts, smoke and/or leather, perhaps something redolent of a farmhand's armpit after a heavy night on the hooch and a roll in the hay?

While our gustatory receptors (taste buds) on the tongue, the walls of the mouth and in the alimentary canal (yes, our stomachs have taste buds too) identify the five primary tastes – salt, sugar, sour, bitter and umami – it is our sense of smell that gives us the critical nuances of whatever we're drinking.

The aromas travel through the nose and the back of the throat to reach our olfactory receptors. These can detect thousands of flavours, which is why what we smell is intricately linked with what we perceive as being taste. Touch is no less important. A glass should sit comfortably in your hand, giving a sense of pleasure from the balance between the weight of the vessel and the liquid it contains. When that liquid hits your lips it should do so with as little interference as possible, and this is where the rim comes in. Take a nice wine glass and pour in a drink – anything, even water, will do – then taste it. Do the same with a jam jar and you'll see what I mean. Jam jars should only be used for jam, pencils or tadpoles, regardless of what the hipsters say.

Just as eating from a wobbly paper plate with a plastic knife and fork somehow diminishes the pleasure of the food in question, so drinking from an inadequate vessel will lessen the pleasure of your chosen libation. Plastic's kind of fine for a picnic (though it's so easy to sling in some sturdy tumblers wrapped in a couple of tea towels, it seems unnecessarily masochistic, not to say expensive and environmentally irresponsible, to pick plastic instead) but there's something rather mean about them when they hit your lips. Also, they are wont to crack, with disastrous consequences, should you grip them too firmly. Paper's also okay in an emergency, though it has a tendency to go floppy after a while when a firm grip can also lead to unfortunate spillage.

As for sound? Most of us recognise our own Pavlovian responses to the sound of ice clinking in a glass, the jolly 'psst' as we open a can of tonic or the arousing pop as we tease the cork from a bottle of champagne, and there is science to prove that sounds do indeed get our digestive juices flowing. Light and tinkling music will heighten sweet and creamy sensations while deep and mellifluous music will enhance the bitter and the dry. The volume of background noise has an effect too – a staggering 27 per cent of all drinks ordered on aeroplanes are tomato juice (with or without vodka). The 80 or so decibels of noise in an aircraft's cabin interferes with our ability to taste sweetness, while it enhances our perception of savoury umami, so makes the tomato juice taste extra good. Tannins and acidity are also more pronounced in a pressurised cabin flying at 30,000 feet, why I never drink wine on aeroplanes; if I fancy a little tincture after takeoff I always go for a G&T. A much-travelled and much-lauded bartender sagely said to me, 'As long as there's plenty of ice and the tonic's not Britvic, it's really hard to fuck up.'

At the end of the day, the brain is the only sensory organ we have; how we perceive what we are drinking is all in the mind – literally. The brain takes messages from receptors in all the sensory organs, and filters them through the darkest corners of our memories and personal predilections to give us our 'sense' of what we are drinking. It is so much more than what we see, smell and taste.

There is a famous, much-repeated experiment whereby subjects are given two glasses of wine, one white, one red. They are asked to describe the aromas and tastes of the wines, and to hazard a guess at what they are. The schtick is that they are the same wines, the red one being merely tinted with a tasteless

colouring. The results are consistently extraordinary: those who fancy themselves as wine buffs use words such as 'fresh, crisp, floral' when describing the
white wine (words so frequently found on professional tasting notes), then slip
into 'red fruit, spices, pepper and leather' when they're tasting the red.

Those who have very little experience of drinking wines fare the best –
in one tasting a self-confessed wine hater said immediately, 'they taste the
same to me'. On another occasion a renowned South African winemaker was
given the 'red' first – he was puzzled, certain that it wasn't South African or
even New World, then contemplated it still further and suggested it might be
Italian, possibly from Piedmont. Then he sniffed the white wine and recognised
it immediately. 'That's my wine,' he said. 'I made that.' He'd been smelling and
tasting the same wine.

It is said that the reason we chink glasses to toast when we're drinking
is that the sound completes the full sensory circle. (I'm all for enthusiastic
chinking but a small word of warning here: chink bowl to bowl not rim to rim;
this minimises the danger of breakage and also gives the best ringing noise).
Sight, smell, taste, touch and sound join forces: all the senses are engaged and
are woven together to deliver the full glorious experience of what drinking can
and should be.

3
THE BUILDING BLOCKS

GLASSWARE

I'D LIKE TO RAISE A HUGE GLASS of something lovely to whoever it was, somewhere around 3500BC, probably in Egypt, who looked at a pile of sand and thought: 'Hmm. I wonder what happens if I heat that to an incredibly high temperature, especially if I stir in a bit of potash and/or limestone?'

What happens is a kind of alchemy: the sand melts at around 1700°C/3092°F and becomes a clear-ish liquid that undergoes a complete transformation of its molecular structure and cools to become what we now call glass, a curious substance that is known as an amorphous solid – something with the crystal-line structure of a solid but the molecular randomness of a liquid.

Although our Egyptian and his friends first used glass to make decorative beads, it wasn't long before they were pouring the molten liquid over moulds made from clay to create drinking vessels. It was a slow and laborious process so these early wine glasses were available at vast expense to only the higher echelons of society; it wasn't until the 1st century BC that some bright spark in Phoenicia hit on the idea of blowing through one end of a tube to inflate a lump of molten glass attached at the other and create hollowed-out glassware that could be shaped by the skill of the craftsman to create vessels that were relatively quick and easy to make.

My father was something of a glass collector. The cupboards of my childhood were filled with an array of glassware. There were flutes for fizz, goblets for claret, heavy crystal tumblers for gins and tonic or whisky, straight-sided Victorian rummers, modern burgundy bowls and exquisite Georgian glasses with air-twist stems tiny enough for only a thimbleful of port or perhaps a nip of madeira.

At ostentatious dinner parties each guest would use at least four different glasses throughout the evening – grown-ups in those days tended to run the full gamut of the booze and then drive home. I have fond childhood memories of mornings-after with a multitude of sticky glasses lined up next to the sink. My father would fill a bowl with soapy water, dredge the glasses through it then rinse them under hot running water and set them upside down on a clean cloth he'd laid on the draining board so as not to chip their delicate rims. Then he'd polish each glass lovingly, holding it up to the light, until it sparkled. I spent years watching this ritual – goggle-eyed, transfixed by the glittering beauty of the glint and the gleam, small feet kicking against the twin-tub –

until finally I was allowed to wield the polishing cloth. I have never since felt more adult, more trusted.

The mode of transporting whatever we are drinking into our mouths has a critical bearing on how we relish the whole experience, so it's worth making the effort to get it right. Riedel make glorious glasses, so light and delicate, as do Zalto, whose outré angular shape and improbably fine stem are wonderful to drink from but can be stressful when it comes to the polishing. I speak from bitter (and costly) experience and advise washing such high-end glassware very carefully and only when sober in the cold light of day. For day-to-day drinking I use something more robust that won't make me weep if it gets smashed.

Whatever shape or size you choose, look for something with a fine rim so the liquid makes as seamless a transition from glass to mouth as possible. This is particularly important when drinking wine of any sort; aperitifs knocked up over ice are more forgiving of something rather chunkier and, of course, rims don't really matter if you choose to drink through a straw.

The most important thing to remember is that no glass, whatever its value or beauty, or whatever it holds, is worth drinking out of unless it is gleamingly, dazzlingly clean. Those who know me will attest that I have a pathological obsession with clean glassware, to the point when I will surreptitiously polish my glass with a napkin if they're not to my exacting standards in a restaurant. I try not to do the same if I'm a guest in somebody's house but sometimes even then the compulsion is stronger than my sense of decorum. My brother is the same; our father died when we were in our twenties and we like to think of our condition as him keeping an eye on us from the grave.

There is something almost metaphysically beautiful about a semi-transparent liquid in a perfectly transparent glass, and how the two behave together. How the glass allows the colour and clarity of the liquid to show itself in its best light, and how the liquid clings to the glass and curtseys, showing its metaphorical ankles and sometimes its legs as well. I am not a fan of the domestic dishwasher for washing glasses – with frequent use they leave an unattractive and indelible cloudy film on the glassware, as well as a vile whiff of U-bends, but then I know people who take their glassware very seriously and swear they're fine as long as you wash nothing else with them. Feel free to experiment; I'll be the one at the sink wearing rubber gloves, happily making free with the hot water and suds.

So we come to the matter of the glass cloth for the polishing. Purists (i.e. me) would say a glass cloth should never be used for anything but glasses. It needn't necessarily be made from 100 per cent Irish linen, though these are the cloths my father favoured, but it does need to be made from good-quality linen and/or cotton fibres, tightly woven so that they are smooth enough to leave the required shine while effortlessly absorbing any excess moisture.

The base of the glass, whatever its shape, should be held in the corner of one end of the cloth while its bowl is polished inside and out with the fingers of the other hand in the other end of the cloth. If the glass is large, use two cloths, one in each hand.

There is one exception to the spotless glass rule, though it pains me terribly to say. Glasses for sparkling wine actually profit from a spot of dirt to give the carbon dioxide dissolved in the liquid something to nucleate onto and thus be released as gas. Bubbles will rise one above another from this nucleation point, this stream of bubbles being known as the *perlage*, so I don't polish the very bottom of glasses I'm using for fizz for this very reason. The sides and the rim, of course, get a very good buffing.

GLASSWARE ESSENTIALS

These are the six basic glass shapes that I usually have to hand to get me through the full gamut of aperitif situations. It is something of a luxury to have so many; if I had to choose just one it would be a decent-sized wine glass, in which no drink can go far wrong.

High-balls/hi-balls,Collins glasses
Tall glasses that suit long mixed drinks such as gins and tonic. Some flare out towards the top but I prefer the elegance of those with straight sides, whose slim shape means you can hold them with just the tip of the thumb and one or two fingers, so keeping the glass and its contents as cool as possible, while their narrow mouth keeps the bubbles in place.

Flutes
Synonymous with fizz. Tall, slim and elegant, like the most chic guest at a summer wedding, they hold the bubbles in sparkling wine well, while their narrow mouth concentrates the aromas and the long stem allows you to hold the glass without warming the wine. But drinking fizz from normal wine glasses is fine as well, as long as it's not filled up too far – to one-third and no more; the aromas gather in the space between the top of the wine and the top of the glass, so these are the best choice if you're drinking fizz with any complexity.

Coupes
These saucer-shaped stemmed glasses (supposedly modelled on Marie Antoinette's breasts, or was it Louis XV's mistress, Madame de Pompadour? Citations vary, but who cares? It's a good story) have a certain louche, fur-coat-and-no-knickers retro charm. They are redolent of the days when racing drivers

and footballers drank, smoked and shagged with as much enthusiasm and practised skill as they displayed in their sport; when they would be photographed pouring costly champagne to cascade over a tower of coupes in a disco-filled nightclub, a pretty girl on each side and a twinkle in each eye.

Coupes also hark back to the Jazz Age, of flappers with sharp bobs and red lips shaped like bows, their beaus in bold blazers and boaters. They certainly make me come over a bit Sally Bowles when they contain a straight-up cocktail ('Divine decadence, darling') but they fall short when it comes to anything fizzy because their wide mouth and shallow shape mean the bubbles disappear very quickly along with the aromas, so much of the fizz and flavour are lost. A cocktail such as a Gin and It is where it's at in a coupe, or any well-chilled cocktail served straight up – in other words, with no added ice.

Tumblers, rocks and Old Fashioned glasses

Short, squat and without a stem, tumblers are thought to be so called because originally, stemless drinking vessels had slightly curved bases so they'd roll a little when placed on a surface, in danger of spilling the drink they contained. These days they tend to be flat-bottomed so are rather safer, and can be used for anything served neat or over ice, with or without a mixer. I use small ones for sips of something straight; larger ones if ice is involved.

Wine glasses

Or 'stemware', as we are supposed to call them. I'm all for drinking rustic vino out of a school-dinner tumbler, especially if one's rolling in the grass at a sun-kissed picnic, or necking *vin de sous la table* in a Marseillaise backstreet, but if the wine is anything more than a notch above your average plonkage it really deserves a stem. Wine pros can get quite neurotic about the precise contours of the glass – the bulbous/slender Bordeaux/Burgundy shapes that supposedly make the wine hit the back/front of the tongue first, so allowing us to best appreciate the full-bodied/delicate nature of the wines, for example – but let's not get distracted by such geekery here. A wine glass should simply be large enough to hold enough wine to enjoy with enough room left over (at least two-thirds) to maximise the swirling/sniffing/ooh-look-at-those-lovely-legs potential. If the sides curve in slightly towards the rim, so much the better. The legs, by the way, are the clear streaks that appear on the inside of the glass, formed as the liquid drips down and the alcohol begins to evaporate from it.

Cocktail glasses

V-shaped glasses with stems, also known as Martini glasses, are best known for housing Martinis and other straight-up cocktails. Elegant, with pleasing lines reminiscent of the art deco aesthetic, cocktail glasses definitely have a place in the keen drinker's armoury, but I have to admit I rarely use them at home. It is another matter altogether in a decent cocktail bar; here they are positively essential. Suffice to say, if your Martini (or other straight-up drink) is not served in a chilled glass, you should move on forthwith; if your half-drunk Martini is transferred to a freshly chilled glass without your noticing, you should tip the bartender handsomely and ask him or her to marry you. This is the kind of attention to detail that marks the great bars from the merely good.

I'm also very partial to V-shaped cocktail glasses without a stem; they're very chic and have the added advantage of being less easily knocked over in situations of extreme merriment.

A word on 'novelty' vessels for your drinks: jam jars are bad enough, but I've also seen drinks served in wellington boots, flowerpots, plastic buckets, tin cans and even (shoot me now) dog food bowls. Just stop.

STRAWS

I blow a bit hot and cold over straws. They caused me no end of joy when I was a child and delighted so in blowing down those twisted candy-stripe paper straws to make my drink bubble in a vaguely suggestive fashion, at least until the straw began to disintegrate and ended up a soggy, useless mess.

Although there is some evidence that drinking through a straw makes you drunk more quickly – the vacuum created when you suck makes the boiling point of alcohol drop, and the vapours created are absorbed into the bloodstream more quickly than when the alcohol in liquid form is absorbed through the stomach – this is not a good reason to adopt straws willy-nilly.

But straws sometimes have their uses: they also serve as stirrers so they often suit a tall drink involving a mixer, and they do away with the danger of the annoying collision between ice cube and nose that may occur. They are also useful for lipstick wearers, for obvious reasons.

Modern plastic straws are virtually indestructible and cause no end of damage to the planet, so use them judiciously. For this reason it is pleasing to see the revival of biodegradable paper straws, more robust than the straws of yore, but they'll still go floppy if you're drinking too slowly. Reusable straws made from stainless steel or other metals are now making an appearance but I'm not keen; metal-on-teeth is an unappetising clash and the metallic taste is impossible to ignore. Bamboo straws may well be the future: they have an eco-warrior worthiness but are relatively neutral in the mouth, and I've heard some bars are starting to grow their own.

GLASSWARE

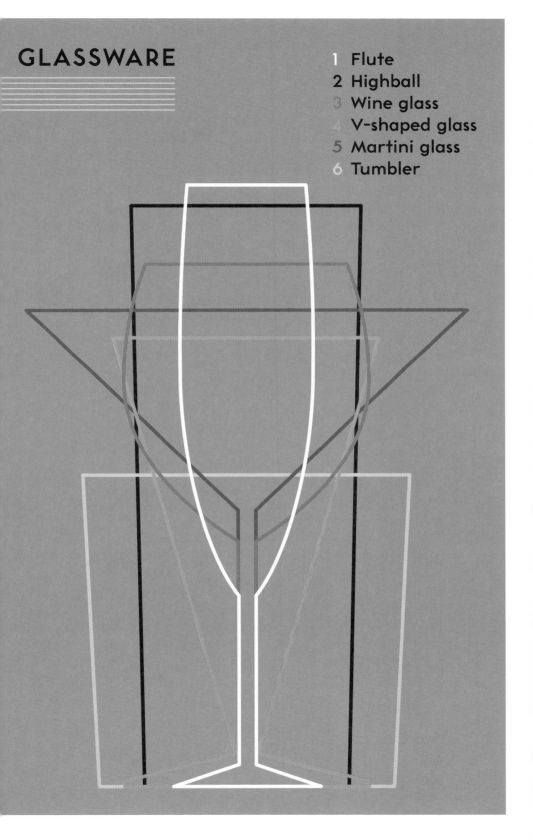

ICE

Ice is important in so many aperitifs – an iceless G&T is quite unthinkable – but in fact it's a relatively recent addition to the European drinking culture.

Aperitifs such as vermouths and other fortified wines would have been drunk *au naturel* in the places they were made, at least until the early years of the 20th century. It was the Americans who first championed ice in drinks by cutting enormous blocks of ice from the frozen wastes of the northern states in the winter and lugging them to the hot and thirsty islands of the Caribbean. By the end of the 19th century machines for making ice were churning out chunks to chill the cocktails enjoyed in America from coast to coast, but the Europeans took a little longer to embrace it. There are several good reasons for the G&T – or anything else involving a fizzy mixer – to be well iced. The jolly clunking of the ice in the glass is just one of them; more scientifically, the lower the temperature, the harder it is for the carbon dioxide dissolved in the drink to escape in the form of bubbles, so the drink will stay fizzy for longer.

Ice obviously chills a drink and also dilutes it to some extent. Some-what counterintuitively, the more ice you add, the less it will dilute the drink because it keeps the volume of the liquid colder so the ice melts more slowly. Geeky cocktail bars often make their own ice, going to great lengths to eliminate impurities in the water by freezing it very slowly to produce crystal-clear blocks of ice that they carve into chunky blocks or sticks. There's no need to be this obsessive at home, although it's worth seeking out ice that comes in large solid cubes without indentations. For those who like a bit of nerdery, you can buy moulds to create ice globes nearly as big as tennis balls that are pleasing to use for something in a tumbler; a friend uses silicone muffin tins to achieve the same effect.

Crushed ice is nice in certain drinks but it melts quickly and is a such a faff to make at home (wrap cubes in a tea towel and bash with a rolling pin, or use one of those handle-operated crushers) that I rarely bother.

SODA

Soda water is carbonated water and appears in so many long drinks it deserves a small mention. Sparkling mineral water will do instead, though beware those like **Badoit** whose salty taste could mar other flavours in your drink. Soda water's job is to be fizzy; don't be tempted to use anything that's gone a bit flat. I swear by my **SodaStream** machine for quality on-tap bubbles: not only does it work out in the long run far cheaper than buying endless bottles, it also cuts out all that worrying plastic waste. The whales will thank you for it in the end.

TONIC

Tonic water plays a critical part in any aperitif drinker's armoury; integral to a G&T of course, but so fitting with many other things besides. What sets tonic apart from other fizzy mixers is its defining ingredient, quinine. Known for its antimalarial properties, quinine comes from the bark of the cinchona tree and is terribly bitter when taken alone. **Schweppes** launched its quinine-based Indian Tonic Water in 1870, inspired by British officers in the days of the Raj who mixed their medicinal quinine with sugar, water and a hefty slug of gin. It is this underlying bitterness that makes tonic such a perfect mixer for vermouths and other similar aperitifs, stimulating the taste buds not deadening them with too much sweetness.

Until not long ago, Schweppes or cheap own-label tonics were pretty much all the choice we had; then **Fever Tree** arrived and has become a global phenomenon. More recently a slew of 'artisan' tonics have hit the market, many making much of their 'natural' ingredients; some flavoured with all sorts of other things as well as quinine. I, along with many professional booze-hounds I know, still prefer Schweppes over others, especially their new '1783' range of premium tonics that have done away with artificial sweeteners. I have researched this extensively and have come to the conclusion that the quality of the bubbles is as important as the taste. Schweppes' bubbles are small and tight so give the best fizz on the tongue, but there are plenty of drinkers out there who'd disagree with me, so who am I to preach?

A NOTE ON...

MEASUREMENTS

Proportions are more important than quantities when mixing a drink. Most bars serve 25ml or 35ml as a single measure for spirits, using a metal measuring cup called a jigger. It's a useful tool for any serious drinker, though a modestly sized egg cup would do at a pinch. If I'm drinking just one spirit with a non-alcoholic mixer, anything less than 50ml/2oz generally seems to be missing the point; in the case of cocktails with several ingredients – Negronis spring to mind – those measures can amount to a hefty thwack of hooch which may not always be entirely sensible. I often use the cap of the bottle – around 10ml – to deliver a drink with the right balance that won't make me fall over.

With aperitifs containing less alcohol – fortified wines and their various cousins – I favour something around 75ml/3oz as a decent amount if I'm drinking it alone, perhaps somewhat less if it's mixed with other things, but it all depends on time, place and current mood.

Measuring individual drinks can be a bit fiddly if you're making more than just a few; you can pre-mix pretty much anything as long as it doesn't have a fizzy mixer or fresh ingredients that might go manky. Sling the ingredients into a jug, then pour into an old wine bottle (or bottles) and keep in the fridge until you're ready to drink. Top tip if you're having a party.

GARNISHES

I'm not a fan of outlandish and unnecessary garnishes; whatever is there should be doing a job beyond its appearance. Citrus fruits so often suit – as a slice or a wedge if you want some juice, or a strip of the skin (without any of the bitter white pith beneath it) for the concentrated zest of its oils. Whichever you use, squeeze it slightly as you drop it into the glass to release its magic. I'm sometimes partial to a sprig of a herb, most often mint, rosemary, basil or thyme, and I like cucumber sliced very fine with a vegetable peeler in some drinks if the weather's warm. My fridge usually has jars of green olives, cocktail onions and griotte cherries; they're nice to have about me but, to be honest, I could live without them if I had to. For me, aperitifs should speak of themselves and do not need anything else too outré to shine.

A FEW OF MY FAVOURITE THINGS...

It will come as no surprise that I have drunk too many aperitifs in my time to remember them all. In my selfless research for this book, however, I have kept a meticulous record. A few horrors stand out that I'd rather forget; others were perfectly pleasant but I'd probably give them the cold shoulder if our paths crossed again. Below is a list of some classic brands that can never put a foot wrong when used in the right context, as well as newer discoveries that particularly caught my fancy. The list is, of course, by no means exhaustive. I urge you to experiment and see what suits you best. If you really don't like a bottle you've bought, use it for cooking in place of wine and continue to search for one that you do.

ITALY
Bērto
Bonmè
Campari
Carpano Antica Formula
Cinzano
Cocchi
Cynar
Del Professore
Martini & Rossi
Mauro Vergano
Punt e Mes
Luigi Spurtino

SPAIN
Barbadillo
Casa Mariol
El Bandarra
Fernando de Castilla
Gonzalez Byass
La Luna
Lacuesta
Lustau
St Petroni

FRANCE
Byrrh
Dolin
Dubonnet
Lillet
Mattei Cap Corsa
Noilly Prat
Rinquinquin
Suze

SOUTH AFRICA
Caperitif

UK
Asterley Bros
Blackdown Silver Birch
Sacred

USA
Ransom
Sutton Cellars
Vya

AUSTRALIA
Regal Rogue

GERMANY
Belsazar
Ferdinand's
Mondino

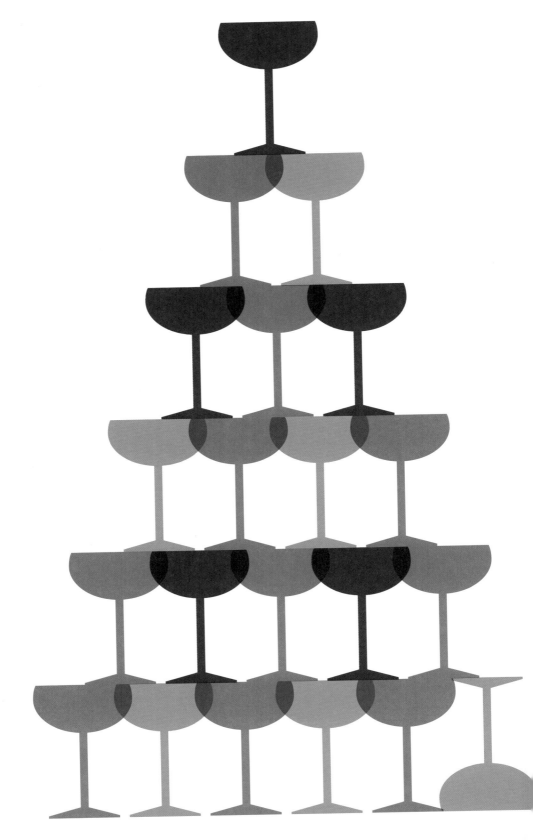

4
THE DRINKS

HOW WINE IS MADE

At its most basic, wine is simply grape juice that is fermented by the action of yeasts – microorganisms that are either naturally whizzing around in the air of the winery or are inoculated into the wine juice by the winemaker – that feed on the sugar in the fruit and give off alcohol in return. Winemaking goes back to around 6000BC, most probably in the Caucasus region in what is now Georgia. Some winemakers there still use the same ancient technique of fermenting grapes and their juice in huge terracotta vessels called *qvevri*, and very fine their wines can be, but of course technology has come a long way and most wine is now made in industrial quantities in industrial wineries.

The process is much the same, though the vessels are usually serried rows of stainless steel tanks taller than a house: grapes are pressed and their juice and sometimes their skins are fermented in the tank. Sometimes the resulting wine may be transferred to oak barrels to lend structure and a whiff of wood as it ages; sometimes the fermentation might happen in the barrel as well as the ageing.

This is not a wine book so it's neither the time nor place to elaborate further on the vast and complicated subject of wine and winemaking. Suffice it to say wine may be made in all manner of vessels including clay, wood, stainless steel, concrete and goat skins, or a combination thereof, and may be treated to more or less 'intervention' at any stage of its making, from spraying the vines with herbicides and pesticides in the vineyard to adding oak chips, acidifiers, sweeteners, colourants, sulphur, charcoal, fish bladders or any of the other 50-plus permitted additives during the winemaking process.

Wines that are made with minimal intervention – so-called 'natural' wines – are not necessarily better or morally superior (some can be quite filthy) to those made more conventionally; many of these additives are there for good reason, to stabilise, clarify and preserve, and without them the overall quality of what we drink would be a lot poorer.

HOW SPIRITS ARE MADE

Spirits, by which we mean alcohol that is distilled rather than simply fermented, can be made from anything of 'agricultural origin', so the rulebook says. These hard liquors (they start at around 37% abv and can rise much higher) are made pretty much all over the world with whatever grows abundantly nearby – grapes, grains, potatoes, sugar (beet and cane), rice, coconuts, agave, to name just a few.

Grape spirits are made with winemaking's byproducts – the skins, seeds and (sometimes) stems of the crushed grapes – called the pomace. The pomace is

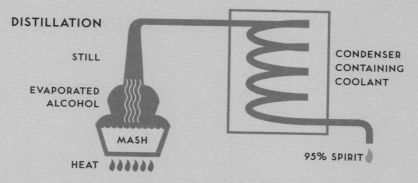

DISTILLATION

STILL

CONDENSER
CONTAINING
COOLANT

EVAPORATED
ALCOHOL

MASH

95% SPIRIT

HEAT

fermented and the resulting gloopy brew, known as the mash, is distilled to create a high-strength spirit that goes by different names depending on where it's made – *grappa*, *eau de vie* and *aguardiente* in Italy, France and Spain, respectively – that still carries a certain grapiness to its flavour along with its bracing alcoholic heat. If the spirit is then aged in oak barrels, it becomes brandy and its various relatives.

Grape spirit is used in many of our favourite aperitifs, as it's what's known as neutral grain spirit – distilled from fermented grains and having no flavour (essentially it's vodka).

Distillation takes place in a piece of equipment called a still. It involves heating the mash until the alcohol in it evaporates and rises as an alcoholic steam, then condenses back into a liquid as it cools at the top of the still. At this point the spirit is at a hair-raising 95% abv or thereabouts, so it is let down with water to something more manageable.

FORTIFICATION

Fortified wines are those that have spirit added to them to preserve and sometimes to impart extra flavour. In the process of fortication, the alcohol kills off the remaining active yeast cells and so fermentation ceases. The unfermented sugars in the wines lend their sweetness to the resulting drink; the earlier the fermentation is stopped, the naturally sweeter it will be.

Sherries, port, madeiras and most sweet wines are fortified with grape spirit and have no additional flavourings; vermouths and other aromatised wines get their distinguishing taste from added botanicals.

Sometimes the spirit is flavoured before being added to the wine, by being either redistilled or infused with the botanicals; sometimes the botanicals are added to the wine which is then fortified with unflavoured spirit.

Judicious use of sugar is important to balance bitterness and also to enhance body and texture. This sweetness may come from sweet wine, or from sugar. Caramel is added to red vermouth to enhance both sweetness and colour.

VERMOUTHS
AND OTHER AROMATISED WINES

Whether you pronounce it VER-muth or the more fashionable, American-influenced ver-MOOTH, vermouth is possibly the most versatile thing you can have in your drinks cupboard (or door of the fridge once it's opened). Made in styles both sweet and dry, all with a backbone of bitterness, vermouths can be sipped alone or mixed with so many other drinks to create wonderful things. Most importantly, it is where the story of aperitifs starts.

Vermouth gets its name from wormwood, a plant found widely in Eurasia and beyond and known for millennia for its medicinal properties; it's so called because it was said to cure intestinal worms. Analysis of drinking vessels from Ancient Egypt and China shows traces of wormwood mixed with wine from the third millennium BC onwards, and herbal wines containing wormwood are found in Ayurvedic texts from India dating back to around 1500BC.

In 5th century BC Greece the father of medicine, Hippocrates, macerated wormwood in wine and prescribed it for jaundice, rheumatism, anaemia and menstrual pains, but it was found to be most efficacious in treating gastric complaints, and it soon became a staple in the medicine cabinets of the classical world as something of a panacea.

As was so often the case, where the clever Greeks blazed a trail, the canny Romans followed. While the lower echelons of Roman society were busy inventing flushing toilets, bureaucracy, concrete and the calendar, the dissolute elite were working hard on perfecting the art of competitive feasting. The Romans were dreadful show-offs and their banquets were preposterously lavish affairs. Guests lounged on cushioned couches as they gorged extravagantly on dishes made from exotic ingredients, the rarer and more costly the better. Delicacies might include peacock brains, flamingo tongues, rabbit foetuses, sow's udders, stuffed dormice and milk-fed snails, washed down with copious quantities of wine (albeit mixed with water) served in ostentatious vessels by oiled-until-glistening nubile slaves. The guests must have been pretty well oiled by the end of the feast as well.

Such horizontal debauchery would have played havoc with one's digestion, so it became customary to take wormwood-infused wine at the beginning of the feast to (open) *apere* the digestive tract and prepare it for the gluttonous onslaught ahead. Wormwood is one of the bitterest substances known to mankind so the Romans, being Romans, added botanicals and expensive spices to make it more palatable. The aperitif was born, and it was a type of vermouth.

Fast-forward through the unrelenting misery of the Dark Ages following the collapse of the Roman empire, when herbalism as medicine was generally practised by monastic orders and warty-nosed crones who frightened the children. Wormwood is found throughout most of Europe so it's likely it was used in concoctions of varying filthiness across the continent but records from this time are scarce – the first printing press didn't appear until 1440 and writing things down must have seemed a bit pointless as nearly all the population were completely illiterate.

Some handwritten texts survive: Pierre-Arnaud de Villeneuve's *Liber de Vinum* (Book of Wine), from around 1320, has a recipe for wine with wormwood and, more significantly, describes the process of distillation to make a spirit that he added to the wine to improve its keeping. This 'fortification' of wine became central to the development of vermouth (as well as so many other aperitifs besides).

In 1555, with printing of books now in relatively full swing, Girolamo Ruscelli, a wine merchant, physician and alchemist otherwise known as Alessio di Piemonte, recorded the results of experiments he'd carried out in Turin with members of his scientific society, the Academy of Secrets, in his *I Secreti*, a compilation of 'excellent remedies against diverse diseases, wounds, and other accidents, with the maner to make distillations, parfumes, confitures, dying, colours, fusions, and meltings'. This has recipes for medicinal wormwood wine and soon he began to market his own concoctions, based on similar things he'd had while travelling in Bavaria and which were known as *wurmut wein*, *wurmut* being the German word for vermouth.

Many families made their own vermouths with whatever herbs and spices they could lay their hands on and recipes were closely guarded, but by 1600 Turin, then the capital of the Duchy of Savoy, was firmly established as the most important centre for vermouth production. Most was sold in concentrated form designed to be diluted with a little wine at home.

The Brits were at it as well. The herbalist Nicolas Culpeper, Puritan and general miserable sod, was sniffy about the Catholic Continentals and their fancy ways with wormwood. In his 1653 book *The Complete Herbal* he recommended steeping wormwood in Rhenish wine but prescribed it strictly for medicinal purposes only, as a remedy for a dull brain and weak sight as well as intestinal worms. His contemporary John French, in his 1651 *Art of Distillation*, used a similar recipe for liver complaints; he also distilled wormwood with urine and other tempting ingredients and swore by it as a cure for dropsy, scurvy, gout and canine wind.

But it wasn't all sackcloth and ashes. In 1659 the famously bawdy Samuel Pepys gave his guests wormwood wine in a Rhenish wine house in London; it's fairly safe to assume he was more interested in it for the effect of its alcohol than for its medicinal qualities. When it came to boozing, the Brits preferred beer (Pepys also refers to wormwood beer, known as 'purl'), so never took to these wines en masse. By the end of the 17th century vermouth, still called wormwood wine, or *eysel* (the term 'vermouth' didn't appear in English until 1806), slipped from whatever favour it had in Britain as people's heads were turned by a new drink brought to their shores by the Dutch-born king William of Orange in 1689. Genever, a spirit distilled with juniper berries, had arrived and so the first British Gin Craze began. It would be more than 300 years until we had the sense to embrace vermouth again. Over on the more civilised Continent, vermouth became something of a craze, to be drunk for enjoyment as well as as a digestive aid.

Modern Italian vermouths can be traced back to 1757 when the **Cinzano** brothers were making a vermouth on a small scale in the remote mountain town of Pecetto in the north of Piedmont, but it was only sold locally so never caused much of a wave among trendsetters. In 1786 herbalist Antonio Benedetto **Carpano** created the first commercial vermouth in Turin, made from good quality moscato wine fortified with alcohol, then sweetened and given its colour with caramel, and called Wurmut as a tribute to the Duchy's German roots. Carpano cannily sent a case to the king, Vittorio Amedeo III, who immediately gave it the royal stamp of approval; French was the main language spoken in Savoy so he named it 'vermouth'. So enamoured was he that he ordered Carpano's vermouth to become the official drink at court, banning the production of the previously favoured **rosolio** (see page 56); thus it became all the rage among the influential and affluent fashionistas. Turin's see-and-be-seen café society adopted with gusto the daily custom of *aperitivo*, a time for socialising with pre-prandial drinks at the city's many watering holes, and Carpano's concoction was more often than not the drink of choice. In 1816 the Cinzanos, doubtless hearing of Carpano's success, moved their operation to Turin where their vermouth became so popular it was soon outselling Carpano's.

The other great stalwart of Italian vermouth-makers, **Martini & Rossi**, was formed in 1863, a partnership of wine merchant Alessandro Martini and Luigi Rossi, a demon herbalist. Martini's enterprising zeal led to rapid expansion of the business and penetration into lucrative export markets made possible by ever-improving transportation links to the rest of the world.

Joseph Chavasse, a distiller from Chambéry in eastern France, then also part of the Duchy of Savoy, visited Turin and saw the vermouth craze in full swing. In 1821 he launched **Dolin Vermouth de Chambéry**, made with local wine and alpine botanicals he had on his doorstep and lighter in style than those made in Turin. Vermouth de Chambéry and Vermouth di Torino (Turin) remain the only geographically protected vermouth styles.

Meanwhile, the Cinzano boys were shipping their vermouth to France where it caught the attention of one Joseph Noilly. Transported in wooden barrels exposed to the sea air during the voyage, the vermouth took on a briny tinge to its taste which Noilly, an absinthe producer from Lyon, found very pleasing; he worked on developing a recipe. In 1813 he set up production of his white, dry style of vermouth in the village of Marseillan on the Mediterranean coast, a technique that involved leaving barrels of fermented wine exposed to the elements for a year or more, during which time some wine would evaporate through the barrel's porous oak, its place being taken by the salty air, which imparted its flavour to the wine. It would then be fortified and steeped with herbs and spice including, *bien sûr*, wormwood.

Joseph handed over the business to his son Louis in 1829 who began exporting to north America with huge success. When Louis's English brother-in-law Claudius Prat joined the family firm in 1843, the name was changed to **Noilly Prat** and the rest, as they say, is history – Noilly Prat is perhaps the most famous and best-loved dry vermouth of them all, and the one favoured by all my favourite bartenders for a classic Martini cocktail.

This is where we get the old-fashioned differentiation of 'French' vermouth, meaning dry and white, while 'Italian' referred to the sweet, red style. These days the lines are more blurred, with red sometimes being made on the dry side and white sometimes sweet.

The diaspora of Italian immigrants to the USA in the 1860s brought vermouth to the lucky Americans. They preferred to drink it with ice and possibly a splash of soda water and news of this exotic habit reached the folks back home. Ice was very scarce in Italy except in winter in the mountains, and even fridges were decades away from becoming the norm; most Italians would have drunk their vermouths at room temperature until well into the 20th century. Giulio **Cocchi**, a pastry chef from Florence, fell in love with a girl from Asti and moved there to be with her. In 1891 he launched a range of vermouths made with the local moscato grape, including what he called Cocchi Americano – meaning made 'to be drunk in the American style', as well as a riff on *amer*, the Italian word for bitter – a lighter style of vermouth predominantly flavoured with gentian that suited this way of serving.

The cocktail craze that (literally) swept America off its feet in the latter years of the 19th century saw vermouth's fortunes rise to the fore. Although Jerry Thomas makes no mention of it in his 1862 book *How to Mix Drinks*, the first guide to cocktails in the English language, by the 1880s vermouth was appearing in many mixed drinks. In 1882 the Democrat newspaper remarked, 'It is but a short time ago that a mixture of whiskey, vermouth and bitters came into vogue'. This cocktail – the Manhattan, equal parts of sweet vermouth and rye whiskey with a dash of orange bitters – is thought to have been invented in the Manhattan Club in New York in 1880 (although, like all cocktails, its origins are debatable). It remains one of the world's classics.

Vermouth also had a fillip when absinthe (another wormwood-based drink that was flavoured with anise) was banned in America in 1912, in France in 1915 and in Italy in 1926, allegedly for making people mad, bans that weren't lifted until later in the 20th century or, in the case of the USA, until 2007. Prohibition of spirit-based aperitifs over 16% abv as part of the French war effort in World War I only saw the fortunes of vermouth and other aromatised wines rise still further.

Cocktails were all the rage on both sides of the Atlantic in the mid-war years, especially following the end of Prohibition in America in 1933, and vermouths both sweet and dry found their way into so many drinks that are still beloved by so many drinkers.

Successful ad campaigns by Martini & Rosso and Cinzano made vermouth as de rigueur as shag-pile carpets and Demis Roussos at all the grooviest parties in the 1960s and '70s, usually drunk long over ice with soda water, tonic or lemonade. But then vermouth fell into something of an unfashionable decline, aside from as a cocktail ingredient, as the millennium drew to a close.

Punt e Mes is a vermouth originally made in Turin by the Carpanos, but now sits under the umbrella of the Branca family in Milan (makers of the famous ultra-bitter **Fernet Branca** digestif). *Punt e mes* means 'point and a half', possibly referring to its having a ratio of one part of sweetness to half a part of bitterness, or then again it might refer to half past one in the afternoon, the traditional time it was drunk as a pre-lunch aperitif.

Today vermouth is in the ascendancy once more, probably traceable to Carpano's incredibly successful relaunch of its **Antica Formula** ('antica' means ancient) in 2001, which hit the new wave of cocktail-making at just the right time. Old vermouth houses have followed suit and launched new or revived vermouths, and new ones are cropping up all over the world.

Although vermouths are fortified, which makes them more stable than unfortified wines, they do start to deteriorate after a while so keep them in the fridge after opening. Delicate white, dry vermouths such as Noilly Prat and the dry Martinis and Cinzanos will lose their delicacy and freshness fastest – I aim to finish a bottle of dry within a fortnight (hardly a great hardship) – while the more robust red and sweeter styles should last a couple of months.

VERMOUTH FROM OTHER PLACES

SPAIN

The Spanish have been making vermouth (there called *vermut*) for well over a century and are some of its most enthusiastic drinkers. Vermouth was first imported from Italy via the docks at Barcelona in the mid-19th century and the nearby city of Reus quickly established itself as the centre for Spanish vermut production. Traditionally drunk by men in bars at *la hora del vermut* – after church on Sundays while the women cooked the lunch – vermouth fell out of favour here too in the latter years of the 20th century. Well, up yours, señors; Spanish vermut has undergone a welcome revival, particularly in the trendy bars of Barcelona where *la hora del vermut* now applies almost 24/7. It is now quite common for bars in Barcelona and beyond to make their own vermuts in house and serve them on tap, with the usual Spanish generosity when it comes to pouring. Usually served either neat over ice in a tumbler with a slice of orange and/or an olive, sometimes with a soda syphon on the side, or made long with the addition of lemonade (Spanish lemonade is much less sweet than British or American – half-and-half lemonade and soda water makes a good approximation), vermut has the hipster seal of approval and boutique producers are making some brilliant examples. Look out for **El Bandarra**, **Vermut de Luna** or anything by **Casa Mariol**.

Lacuesta is the Rioja region's best-known vermut maker and down in sherry country they are catching onto the trend as well – González Byass has revived **La Copa**, its 19th-century vermut recipe made with wine from pedro ximenez and oloroso soleras, while the **Lustau** sherry house makes its with amontillado and pedro ximenez, and a brilliant white version with fino and moscatel. At the opposite end of the country in Galicia, makers such as **St Petroni** are producing wonderfully distinctive vermuts from the local grape albariño.

GERMANY

Hildegarde von Bingen, outspoken multitasker *par excellence* of the ecclesiastical Middle Ages who counted Benedictine nun, philosopher, visionary, composer, beer-maker, mystic and pharmacist among her many callings, made a wine infused with wormwood in 12th-century Germany and recommended it for 'detoxification'.

Homespun vermouths – *wurmut weins* – were generally made domestically or only in small batches for sale; despite the very word 'vermouth' coming from the German word for wormwood – *wurmut* – there is no tradition of commercial production in Germany, and until quite recently vermouth was known as something of a tramp's drink as cheap imported brands of dubious quality can be had for only a few euros.

Wurmut weins are still made by some at home, and many trendy bars are now in on the act, making their own to closely guarded recipes. There are also a few new commercial producers worth keeping an eye out for.

Belsazar launched in 2015, making very good vermouths from high-quality German wines fortified with fruit brandies distilled in the Black Forest. I particularly rate its rosé, made from a base of pinot noir, and recommend it served over ice with just a dash of tonic, or as a wet Martini mixed with the Rose Petal Vodka on page 152. **Ferdinand's** is a gin producer in the Saar valley that also makes a very good vermouth, the world's first made from the riesling grape.

USA

The Americans were quite happy with vermouths imported from Europe, first brought to them by Italian immigrants in the 19th century, but now they're really catching on to the trend and making their own. **Vya** vermouth, launched in California in 1998 by the famous Quady winery, was the first New World vermouth to be made, but it took another decade or so for other wine producers to follow suit. Americans play fast and loose with botanicals, sometimes doing away with the wormwood altogether (let's not get into labelling laws here) and concentrating on the 'craft' concept of using local wines and local botanicals. Other brands to look out for include **Atsby, Imbue, Sutton Cellars** and **Ransom.**

AUSTRALIA

The Australians are also leaping aboard the vermouth bandwagon. **Causes & Cures** and **Maidenii** are among the best new Australian vermouths but my favourite is the range from **Regal Rogue**, who use local wines and botanicals plucked from the bush to make fantastic vermouths with bags of cheerful character and less sugar than their European counterparts.

UK

The Brits made wormwood wine, which they called 'eisel', in the 1600s, but it fell out of favour big time when gin became the in thing towards the end of the century. We had to wait 400 years before a new English vermouth appeared in the shape of **The Collector**, created by Jack Bevan at the wonderful Ethicurean restaurant in Somerset in 2012. Jack has since moved on to other projects so, tragically, The Collector has been discontinued, but there are others now made in Blighty that deserve a mention, including **Blackdown Silver Birch, Sacred, Twisted Nose** and **Asterley Bros.**

OTHER AROMATISED WINES

Vermouth belongs to a category of drinks called aromatised wines – wines that are fortified, usually with grape spirit, and flavoured with botanicals. Vermouths must contain at least 75 per cent wine and, of course, its defining wormwood. Quinquinas are also wine-based and must contain quinine in the form of cinchona, though may contain wormwood as well, while americanos in this aperitif context must contain gentian, although there are gentian-based aperitifs that don't define themselves as americanos. Then there are amaros (amari), which may or may not contain wormwood, cinchona and/or gentian but are usually made from a neutral spirit base rather than from one of wine. It's all very confusing.

What unites this fantastic family of drinks, which range from the whisper-light and bone-dry to the deep, dark and very sweet and may be flavoured with so many botanicals apart from those that define them, is their relatively low alcohol content in comparison with spirits, and their incredible versatility. Many are lovely to drink alone, with or without ice, or with tonic or soda, and of course they make great partners with so many other things as well.

QUINQUINAS

Quinquinas are so named because they contain quinine, a bitter compound found in the bark of the cinchona tree. Spanish colonisers in Peru in the 1600s saw that it was successfully used there to prevent and cure malaria. Malaria was endemic in some parts of Europe then, so news spread fast across the continent on their return. Over the following centuries the bark was dried then ground to a powder and added to wine, but it wasn't until two French scientists isolated quinine as the active ingredient in 1820 that it became widely available. Quinine was an invaluable tool as Europeans marched across the world building their empires in the inhospitable and malaria-ridden tropics, and remained the primary drug used against the disease until well into the 20th century.

The Brits took their quinine as droplets in their beloved gin or, far more agreeably, in the tonic waters with which they mixed it that took off at the end of the 18th century. The French, already keen makers and drinkers of vermouth, added quinine to their aromatised wines, giving rise to iconic quinquinas that still survive.

Dubonnet was the first off the mark. The French government had launched an appeal for a product that would make the anti-malarial but intensely bitter quinine more palatable for the Foreign Legionnaires stationed in North Africa. Joseph Dubonnet came up with the goods in 1846. Originally called 'Quinquina Dubonnet', it perked up the thirsty soldiers no end and soon became the *apéritif du jour* for polite society *dans tous les cafés* in France as well.

Dubonnet was known to be the late British Queen Mother's tipple of choice; she drank it on the dot of noon every day mixed over ice with twice as much gin and a slice of lemon, and her daughter is said to be equally partial. Dubonnet is referenced by artists as diverse as Sylvia Plath, Barbra Streisand, Lou Reed and Mötley Crüe, and if it was good enough for Harry Palmer in *The Ipcress File*, it was good enough for Mary Taylor in *Coronation Street*. Yet these days it tends to gather dust at the back of the drinks cabinet, sadly forgotten and rarely touched. This is a shame; it makes a fine aperitif over ice, with or without the gin, with its light fruitiness, woody spice and modest 15% abv. Rouge is the most commonly available, but it also appears in Blanc and Gold forms.

Byrrh (pronounced 'beer') was born in 1866, the brainchild of Simon Violet, a shepherd from Thuir in the foothills of the Pyrenees, who took wine made from grapes that are local to the Roussillon region, spiked it with chincona then aged it gently in oak to give it some subtle backbone. It has a cherry-tinged fruit with pleasing chocolate and orange notes and wears its quinine bitterness lightly; treat it as you would a sweet vermouth.

Lillet, Bordeaux's first and only aperitif, first appeared in 1872 and is still one of the world's favourites. Kina Lillet (the 'kina' being a reference to the quinine it contained) was specified by James Bond in the making of the famous Vesper cocktail. Now called Lillet Blanc as it's made with less quinine (or none, depending on whom you read), it was also Dr Lecter's favourite aperitif, served over ice with a slice of orange, in Thomas Harris's novel *Hannibal*. I don't have a taste for human flesh but would agree with the good (bad) doctor on this. Lillet also comes in rosé and red versions; both have their own delicate charms and are good served the same way.

St Raphael was invented by Dr Ademar Juppet in Lyon in 1830, whose experimentations in developing it in the dim light of his lab had led to him losing his sight. He prayed to St Raphael, who had cured Tobias of blindness in the Bible, as he perfected the recipe, and lo! his sight returned.

Wine fortified with spirit and infused with botanicals including cinchona, vanilla, cocoa and bitter oranges, St Raphael comes in white (known as *ambré*) and red (*rouge*) forms and these days is hard to find but is worth tasting as an aperitif on ice if you spot it on a bar somewhere.

Barolo Chinato is the Italian take on quinquina, in which the cinchona and other botanicals are macerated in spirit then added to a base of barolo wine and aged in oak barrels for at least a year. **Cocchi** makes a very good one, as does **Borgogno**.

Caperitif The discovery of vast reserves of gold, minerals and precious stones in South Africa at the end of the 19th century led to an influx of intrepid and ambitious prospectors from all over the world. There was big money to be made, and those who struck lucky had it in spades. Those who made their fortunes liked to brag of their success; a feverishly glamorous party scene evolved where cocktails were the order of the day and decadence the order of the night.

Inspired by European vermouths, the Grand Quinquina Caperitif was born, using local chenin blanc wine and botanicals gathered from around the Cape, including quinine and wormwood. It was a smash hit and soon, with typically South African coals-to-Newcastle chutzpah, Caperitif was being exported to Europe where it became terribly fashionable, even getting a mention in Harry Craddock's *Savoy Cocktail Book* of 1930.

Production ceased in 1940 and the recipe disappeared into the annals of bartenders' mythology, but it has recently been revived by Danish bartender Lars Lyndgaard Schmidt and Adi Badenhorst, a maverick South African winemaker who does wild and wonderful things with grapes. After hundreds of experiments they launched the new Caperitif in 2016 as a beautifully balanced semi-sweet aperitif with slightly burnt (in a good way) orange marmalade notes along with a savoury depth and a bitterness of exotic barks from the bush. Whether it bears any relation to the original remains to be seen: three bottles of 1940 Caperitif recently came up for auction in Yorkshire and Badenhorst snapped them up. The plan is to have a ceremonial tasting at the Savoy but a date is yet to be set. Rest assured I am prepared to kill for an invitation.

AMERICANOS

Americanos may or may not contain quinine and/or wormwood but are characterised by having gentian as their dominant battering agent. They were developed by Italian vermouth makers in the 19th century to suit their American customers who liked to take their aperitifs with ice and soda. They tend to be lighter and more floral than vermouths and quinquinas.

(The Americano is also, confusingly, a cocktail – a mix of sweet vermouth, Campari and soda water that has the distinction of being the first drink ever ordered by James Bond, in Ian Fleming's first Bond book, *Casino Royale*.)

Cocchi Americano, still made to the original 1891 recipe, is fragrant with elderflower and orange-peel notes and has a pleasing background sweetness. Some say it's very close to Lillet's original 'Kina', so use it in a Vesper cocktail in place of Lillet Blanc.

Cocchi Rosa is an americano made from a red wine base and has wonderful tinges of saffron and roses.

Contratto Americano Rosso is made by the Contratto winery, known to be the oldest producer of sparkling wine in Italy. Ginger, mint, liquorice and sage sit comfortably around its gentle bitterness.

Suze deserves a mention here just because it's so delicious and quite singular in its charms; it's also something of well-kept secret in serious drinking circles. Invented in 1885 by Ferdinand Moureaux in France and allegedly named after his sister-in-law Susanne (did he have a crush on her, one wonders?), Suze has a thrilling, almost luminous yellow colour that takes your breath away. Made with a wine base and flavoured predominantly with gentian, Suze is sweet like the heady scent of jasmine on a languid night in the tropics but with a thrilling bitterness that develops on the palate into something incredibly savoury and seductive. It also comes in one of the most beautiful bottles one could wish for, and in the world of beautifully packaged aperitifs, that's saying a lot. Drink it straight from the fridge, on the rocks or lengthen it with a splash of soda or tonic. Hell, use it in a Martini, wet or dry, in place of vermouth, or make a White Negroni as on page 113.

OTHER WINE-BASED APEROS WORTH MENTIONING

Rinquinquin Just say the word 'rinquinquin' and you know you're in for a good time. *Très, très* French and *très, très délicieux*, rinquinquin is made in Provence and gets its name from the Provençal verb *requinquilhar*, meaning to 'cheer up' or 'invigorate'. It is made from three different kinds of peaches picked at the peak of ripeness and macerated with their stones and leaves in white wine and grape spirit, then blended together unencumbered by any other flavourings and aged in oak barrels for six months or so. When I was a child I had a friend whose father was a test pilot on the then-nascent Concorde. He'd bring back trays of peaches on his flights back from the French base in Toulouse, the likes of which 1970s Bristol had never seen; their scent and flavour completely captivated me and still live vividly in my mind. It is rare these days I eat a peach as good as those whose juices dripped down my chin and onto my vile green school uniform in the back of the car, but Rinquinquin always reminds me of them – it's the very essence of perfect peachiness. Buy a bottle and you'll see what I mean. It's lovely by itself very cold over ice, or added to a glass of boring sparkling wine for a take on a Bellini.

Pineau des Charentes is the aperitif of the Charentes region of south west France and is said to have been invented accidentally in 1589 when a winemaker added new wine to a barrel he thought was empty but actually contained a little local *eau de vie*. He shoved the barrel into a dark corner of the cellar and hoped nobody would notice, then some years later the barrel was opened and found to contain a very fine drink.

Pineau, as it's simply known here, must be made from grapes grown in the Cognac region, most famous for its brandy of the same name. Young Cognac brandy is used to fortify the unfermented grape juice immediately after pressing, then it's left to age in barrels for 18 months or more.

Made in both white and red styles, pineau tends to be on the sweet side of the aperitif spectrum, but it has good acidity and a certain fragrant charm. Chill it and drink it in a wine glass unhindered by ice; if you happen to have a slab of *pâté de foie gras* to hand, it would make a terribly decadent match. It's also very, very good with slices of ripe chanterais melon.

Floc de Gascogne is Armagnac's version of pineau des charentes, taking its name from *lou floc*, meaning 'bouquet of flowers' in the Gascon dialect. White or rosé, or sometime red, it's fortified with armagnac brandy.

Troussepinette is the Vendée area's riff, made with sloe berries in a red wine base, while **Macvin** from the tiny Jura region in north-east France is made by boiling grapes and must of the local savagnin grape and fortifying it with brandy, and is more usually taken there as a pudding wine or digestif.

Ratafia is the name for the same kind of thing made in Champagne and Burgundy and is drunk in the same way as a chilled aperitif. It's not to be confused with Italian *ratafia* (from the Abruzzo and Molise regions, made in a similar way with local wine but including cherries and other flavourings in the mix), or the Spanish *ratafia* from the south of Catalunya, which is a maceration of green walnuts and other herbs and spices in grape spirit), or indeed the almond essence, or the almond-flavoured biscuits of the same name.

Ratafia, by the way, is thought to get its name from the Latin *ratafiat*, meaning 'the deal is made' (as in to 'ratify'), presumably because it was drunk to toast contracts being signed. Or does it come from the 17th-century Creole *tafia*, a drink made from sugar cane?

Marsala is a fortified wine from Sicily, made in the town from which it gets its name. It dates from 1770 when an English merchant named John Wood-house was passing through the region and noticed the similarity of its wines with those at the heart of his beloved ports, sherries and madeiras. He added local grape spirit and shipped it back to England where it was met with much appreciation. Marsala is made into styles both sweet (*dolce*) and dry (*secco*) and is aged in oak barrels before being bottled. I often keep a bottle of *secco* in my fridge to slosh into meaty dishes and into my glass while I'm cooking them.

AMARI

Amaro is the Italian word for 'bitter' and also the name of the family of bitter drinks the Italians do so well. Unlike vermouths, which have to contain at least 75 per cent wine, amari are generally made with neutral grain alcohol so are treated as a separate category.

Most amari are drunk as digestifs, their bitterness lurking beneath a dark and sticky sweetness that would kill the appetite of any civilised drinker (looking at you, Fernet Branca, the darkest, dirtiest and bitterest of them all), but there are a few that shine as aperitifs and deserve our attention here.

CAMPARI

I was sitting at a table outside a busy café in an elegant, colonnaded square in Turin. Pleased I'd resisted the lure of the leather trouser the Italians so adore and bought instead some rather gorgeous boots, soft as butter and on the dangerous side of high, I sat with my face to the warmth of the late-afternoon autumn sun and ordered (what else?) a Campari Soda.

A man strolled up, sleek but not oily – unpressed jeans, sharp shirt and a cream linen jacket, vintage Ray-Bans and very good shoes with laces not tassels – and asked me (I think; he spoke in Italian) if he could join me as all the other tables were occupied. He ascertained my Englishness and poor grasp of Italian; fortunately he was fluent in both. 'Nice boots,' he said, as a waiter appeared bearing a Campari Soda on a tray. Turned out he stopped by this bar whenever he was in town (he was a 'businessman', he told me) and always drank the same. He – Alessio – brought the glass to his lips, looked me in the eye and said softly, 'Ah, bellissimo Campari. The colour of sin; the taste of the fiendish'. I was putty in his well-manicured hands.

We ordered another and talked of how we both adore it. Some people hate Campari because they can't stand the bitterness; for Campari lovers, that's just what we like. We love the come-to-bed redness of a good Campari Soda, its seductive bittersweetness lifted with just enough bubbles to quench the thirst. Out of all the other amari, we agreed that Campari was where our true hearts lie. Halfway down our third I started to get my words mixed up, I heard myself talking of *amore* (love) instead, and I blushed to the bottom of my blue suede boots. Oh god. Alessio leaned over and whispered, 'I'm driving to my place in

Milan tonight; why don't you join me?' Oh, Alessio.

I came to my senses just in time and realised it was the Campari and not Alessio that had seduced me. I had a dinner date with some friends, I explained, and needed to get back to my hotel. 'Let me take you; I'd like to take you,' he purred. 'For fuck's sake, Alessio,' I whispered under my breath.

We strolled around the corner and there was his car – a baby-blue soft-top E-type Jaguar, cream leather seats and a walnut dashboard, almost a perfect match with my new boots. *Bellissimo*, indeed. I slipped into the passenger seat as gracefully as I could, given that the boots had started pinching and the Campari had rendered me a bit wobbly. We drove in the orange-tinged dusk down Turin's lavish avenues and boulevards, past piazzas and palazzos, crossing and re-crossing the sultry river Po on its ancient bridges, until we arrived at my hotel. I think he took the long way round. A chaste kiss as we said goodbye, then he handed me an embossed business card, nice and stiff.

'*Ciao, bella.*'

I still have the card, ten years later, and the wonders of the Internet now reveal that, no word of a lie, dear Alessio was caught speeding in the self-same Jag just weeks afterwards; he'd been on the run and was later charged with tax evasion and drug offences. I suspect this just goes to show that Campari appeals to the devil in us all.

Campari was invented by master mixologist Gaspare Campari in Milan in 1867 to serve in his modest bar Caffe Campari in the centre of the city. As luck would have it, the bar was on the site of the proposed Galleria Vittorio Emanuele II, so Signore Campari had first dibs on a spot when the grand shopping arcade was built shortly afterwards. He plumped for a corner spot at the entrance to the arcade; with such a prime location Campari's bar became the place to see and be seen and his eponymous drink was what Milan's fashionistas wanted to be seen drinking. In 1915 he opened another bar, Il Camparino, directly opposite Caffe Campari, which featured a terribly modern hydraulic system delivering chilled soda water from the cellar directly to the bar. Campari with soda was thus established as Milan's signature *aperitivo* and so it remains. Il Camparino is still there in Milan, and so are the fashionistas drinking Campari.

Gaspare's lovestruck but financially astute son Davide was inadvertently responsible for Campari's success abroad. He had fallen desperately in love with a beautiful opera singer and flattered her by featuring her portrait on Campari's early advertising. So in love with her was he that he followed her to Nice, then to Moscow and New York, taking his father's aperitif with him on the pretext he'd sell it to the foreigners. He failed to win her heart each time but succeeded in making Campari the bestselling amaro in the world by the mid-1930s. He understood the power of design and branding and employed famous artists and filmmakers to create evocative advertisments, but his real stroke of genius was to market his drink as an aperitif served long; other amari at the time were generally drunk only as digestifs after eating.

Then, as now, the exact blend of the 68 botanicals that give Campari its distinctive colour and taste – 'cryptically bitter' as it was marketed in 1960s ads – is a closely guarded secret known only to the company's current president. At Il Camparino they serve their Campari Sodas in tall glasses with short stems; the Campari, soda water and glasses are all kept chilled so ice is not required. This has the added advantage of not diluting the drink beyond its optimum concentration.

Campari Soda should be drunk at roughly 50:50 Campari and soda water, perhaps a little less Campari if you're not adding ice – if you dilute it too much you will lose the perfect balance of the bitterness and sweetness. The soda must be fizzy – any sparkling water will do, but don't be tempted to use anything that's been open for a while and has lost its pizzazz. Most bars and restaurants in the UK or US serve it over-diluted, so be clear when you order exactly how you'd like it served – I quite often ask for the soda to be served alongside so I can dilute it exactly to my taste. I can almost hear the bartender's eyes rolling and I can sympathise. Forgive them, Lord, for they know not what they do.

Any glass is fine really, but ideally it should be served in a long glass, and over ice if, as in most bars, the Campari is not kept chilled. I favour giving it a quick stir then drinking it directly from the glass rather than through a straw, and I prefer a slice of lemon over the more traditional orange.

At home I am rarely without Campari and soda water in my fridge, so there I tend to make it with little or no ice. I think Alessio would approve: undiluted sin. Campari has a natural affinity with oranges – try it with freshly squeezed juice, preferably from blood oranges – and, of course, it is the defining ingredient in a Negroni (see page 113), as well as many other cocktails.

APEROL

Those of us *d'un certain âge* remember the world before Aperol. Imagine! In fact, even those young enough to be my children were born before Aperol really hit the international scene in the early 2000s; in that time the Aperol Spritz has become perhaps the most famous Italian aperitif of them all.

Created in Padua in Italy's Veneto region in 1919, Aperol took a while to take off. Flavoured with orange, rhubarb and gentian, sweeter and less bitter than Campari and bottled at only 11% abv (compared to Campari's 25%), Aperol was originally targeted at women and those of a sporty persuasion to help them stay 'lean and fit'. When some bright spark invented the Aperol Spritz in 1950 and tagged its simple 3:2:1 recipe (three parts white wine, two parts

Aperol, one part soda water) onto its advertising, its fortunes began to look up, although it was still very much a well-kept Italian secret until much later.

The Campari group acquired Aperol in 2003 and threw massive marketing budgets at it with impressive success. Reviving the Aperol Spritz was the key – it was a light, easy-to-drink aperitif that seemed very modern but had a reassuring Italian heritage behind it; it has a whiff of sophistication along with its distinctive radioactive orange colour that leaves nobody in any doubt as to what they're drinking.

The Aperol Spritz is a mainstay of *aperitivo* hour for Venetians and their tourists – it is estimated that around 300,000 are drunk there every day. The original Venetian spritz was always made with local white wine and either Campari, Aperol or another local amaro called Select. This would be served in a large tumbler, topped with soda water and served with a slice of lemon and an olive. Elsewhere in Italy the spritz was generally served in a large wine glass with prosecco used instead of still wine, an orange slice replacing the lemon and the olive removed altogether. Other amari became seen as deviant; it had to be Aperol. Now most places in Venice make it this way as well – simply ask for *uno spritz* and it's bound to be made with Aperol, although few diehard bars still make their spritzes in the traditional fashion.

The Campari-loving (and rather snobbish) Milanese think of Aperol as somewhat 'chavvy', according to a specialist I know, and somebody (well, me in fact) rudely calls it 'Campari for girls'. Given the choice, I'd have a spritz made with Campari instead (less sweet and with a classier colour), but having said that I've never been known to kick an Aperol Spritz out of bed for leaving crumbs, as it were.

The simple 3:2:1 recipe works well, though I sacrilegiously use cava given the choice as it's less sweet than prosecco. A large wine glass with plenty of ice is the classic serve, though I prefer a workmanlike tumbler and, as with Campari Soda, I go easy on the ice.

CYNAR (CHEE-NAR)

Cynar is the relatively new kid on the amaro block – it's only been around since the 1950s – but it's one that has stolen many hearts and is now one of the world's bestselling amari. Named after cynarina, an extract from the leaves of artichokes (globe not Jerusalem) with which it's made, Cynar has a particular kind of bitterness, almost medicinal but lifted with tantalising bitter orange fruit, and unlike the look-at-me bright colours of Campari and Aperol, it comes in a rather unassuming brown.

Russell Norman of the Polpo restaurant group in England can take a large chunk of the credit for putting Campari and other amari into the trend-setters' spotlight. 'Campari is the everyday choice,' he tells me conspiratorially.

'But best of all is Cynar. It's the bitter of choice in the spritz of the aficionado.'
If it's good enough for Russell, it's good enough for me.

FERNET BRANCA

Mention should be made here of Fernet Branca. Fernets were originally made by hermits living high in the Alps using extracts they made from the hardy plants growing around them; whether they were made for pleasure or for penance is unclear.

The Branca family launched their own fernet in Milan in 1845; today it has something of a 'specialist website' appeal among seasoned drinkers, at least in Europe. Generally taken as a digestif, traditionally with a splash of hot water, it's also renowned as a hangover cure, especially when mixed 2:1 with crème de menthe into what's called a Dr Henderson, a recipe given to chef Fergus Henderson by his father. Don't knock it till you try it; it makes me feel slightly depraved but I have a perverse fondness for this drink.

When it comes to Fernet Branca as an aperitif, in San Francisco they apparently serve it mixed with ginger ale and call it a Bartender's Handshake, while down in Argentina fernet mixed with Coca Cola (*fernet con coca*) is virtually the national drink; Fernet Branca set up a factory there to keep up with the demand, and this is why the Argentinians drink four times as much Coca Cola per head than the global average. I think it's pretty revolting but who am I to say? Perhaps it's better in a bar in Buenos Aires than it is in Bristol. And I have it on good authority from a friend I trust that it beats even a Dr Henderson on mornings after the night before.

There is definitely something to be said for time and place, and this has reminded me. Rum and Coke is something I'd never, ever order in a bar, and I'm rather horridly scornful of it and those who drink it – it's an over-sweet confection for those too unsophisticated to know any better. Call it a Cuba Libre, however, and serve it with a lot of lime juice and plenty of ice on a sultry night in a backstreet bar in Havana and it suddenly becomes EXACTLY what I want.

MONDINO

Made in Germany with Bavarian botanicals, Mondino is lighter than Campari and is a joy with just a splash of soda water or in a Negroni with a vermouth without too much attitude.

PICON

One of the more unlikely of the many jobs I've had was for a well-known English cider company to research how well their sweet fizzy cider might go down in the bars of Paris. I could probably have told them the outcome before I left, but I was being paid to spend a week in Paris so thought I'd better go, just to check.

The job involved visiting dozens of bars each day to observe what they were serving and who was drinking it. There is a limit to the number of *petits cafés* a girl can drink without getting twitchy, or the number of *verres d'eau* before she gets bored. Wine makes me sleepy and doesn't quench the thirst, and pastis was out of the question for obvious reasons. It was here I discovered Picon Bière, which hit the spot with a bullseye.

Picon is one of the happier outcomes of the French involvement in North Africa. Gaetan Picon, a French soldier stationed in Algeria, created his drink in 1830 and called it Amer Africain, *amer* meaning 'bitter' in French as it does in Italian. Made with gentian, orange peel and the essential quinine against the ever-present threat of malaria, Picon's drink proved a proper tonic for the troops and he set up a distillery in the Algerian town of Philippeville in 1837.

He brought it back to France and established a factory in Marseilles in 1872, renaming it Amer Picon. It was received well, particularly in the north of the country where they'd developed a taste for such things mixed with beer. Picon was relaunched in the 1990s as Picon Bière (designed to be mixed with beer) and Picon Club (for adding to wine, as is more popular in the south of France).

Picon Bière is still popular in northern France but it is not considered chic, which is possibly why it was favoured by *les vrais punks* in the glory days of punk rock. Adding a depth of sweetness and a bitter twang, it's best taken to quench the thirst when faced with cheap and horrid lager, either at home or in a scruffy bar, and then only in small quantities – it is famous for bad heads. It gives a touch of *Ça plane pour moi*, as Plastic Bertrand might put it.

ROSOLIO

This is in a category all of its own. Rosolio was first produced by nuns and monks in Florence at a date we'll never know. It was drunk at the court of the Medici in the 16th century when it was made with rose water, cloves, cardamom and cinnamon, and coloured with cochineal made from ground-up beetles.

The Dukes of Savoy were particularly partial and served rosolio at the royal court in Turin where it was known as the 'Aperitivo di Corte' until Vittorio Amedeo III banned its production in favour of Antonio Carpano's new-fangled vermouth at the end of the 18th century.

Having fallen out of royal favour, rosolio continued to be made but only on a domestic scale, each family's recipe being closely guarded by their grandmothers. It was brought out to be served in small glasses on special occasions and celebrations – it was traditional to give it to newlyweds after their marriage, and it was given to guests as a token of good luck.

Rosoli (the plural) are made by macerating a combination of flowers, fruits, spices and herbs in alcohol then diluting with water and sweetening with syrup made from sugar beet. Sugar beet is significant in that it is purer in flavour than sugar from cane so allows the delicate nature of rosolio's botanicals to shine. Cane sugar was brought to southern Europe by the Crusaders – or was it the Arabs? – but it was very labour-intensive to grow and process there so remained very much a luxury 'spice' and was priced accordingly until cheap sugar from plantations in the West Indies and South America arrived in Europe in the 16th century.

Unlike vermouths, rosolio was never intended to a be medicine – it was taken purely for pleasure right from the off, and was soon being made all over Italy. Recipes were inspired by local ingredients, so in the south citrus fruits tended to dominate while the Tuscans used juniper and in Piedmont rose petals were favoured.

In 2016 Giuseppe Gallo, famous Italian mixologist and specialist in vermouth and other aromatised wines, launched Italicus Rosolio di Bergamotto, the first commercial rosolio to be made. Inspired by his own grandmother's recipe, Gallo uses bergamot, rose petals, Sicilian lemons, lavender and lemon balm and the result is a really charming drink, intensely floral and aromatic but quite sweet. Drink it chilled or over ice, or mix it with cheap prosecco for something rather swanky.

SPARKLING WINE

'A single glass of champagne imparts a feeling of exhilaration. The nerves are braced; the imagination is agreeably stirred; the wits become more nimble,' said Winston Churchill, always one for a good booze-related quote. Here he hits the nail on the head when it comes to sparkling wine as an aperitif.

Who would not be cheered by a glass of bubbles? Fizz is short for 'celebration' and puts us in the mood for fun before we've taken our first sip. The jolly 'pop' as the cork comes out is guaranteed to raise a smile and is one of my favourite rituals.

Most sparkling wine has a mushroom-shaped cork held in place with a wire cage called a muselet which is removed by twisting on the wire loop at its base. It always takes exactly six twists to release it. Hold the cork firmly in your left hand and the bottom of the bottle in your right at an angle of about 45 degrees, then twist the bottle, not the cork, until the cork comes out. This is the classy way of doing things: shaking the bottle beforehand will give the famous racing-driver eruption, but that's such a waste of good drink, and very messy besides.

Sabrage is the ostentatious technique of opening a bottle of sparkling wine with a sabre, or any other sword you have to hand. The blunt edge of the weapon is boldly swept up the body of the bottle to shear the collar and the cork away from the neck. It was a method popular with Napoleon's cavalry as they flirted with *champengnoise* aristocracy and is certainly impressive when performed correctly. I've never attempted it with a sabre but have done so with a good kitchen knife; I received rapturous applause but, frankly, I was only showing off.

NOTE ON STYLES OF SPARKLING WINE

Sparkling wines range from the bone dry to the decidedly sweet, depending on how much (if any) sugar is added to the finished wine – what's known as the dosage. These styles are indicated on the label, from the driest to sweetest, thus: Brut nature (or Zero dosage), Extra brut, Brut, Extra Dry, Sec (or Dry), Demi-sec, Doux.

A word of warning to those seduced by sparkling wines marketing themselves as 'low sugar' or 'skinny'. They generally equate to a saving of around 8 calories a glass compared with 'normal' fizz; if you neck a whole bottle, your health should be more worried by the amount of alcohol you've drunk than the piffling extra 50 calories or so.

CHAMPAGNE

Champagne is, of course, the *non plus ultra* of sparkling wine, the benchmark against which all others are measured, the most revered and (generally) the most expensive of all. Champagne is not just a drink, it is a statement of wealth and status. Just as top cuvées attract the attention of our flashiest celebrities today, champagne has always appealed to those with a penchant for glitz – blingtastic Louis XIV was a great fan, as was Marie Antoinette.

The champagne industry guards its lucrative reputation carefully, imposing stringent laws governing how and where it is made in order to be able to call itself the C-word. The Champagne region, surrounding the towns of Reims, Epernay and Ay in northeast France, was originally famed for its pale-pink still wines, usually made from pinot noir.

Sparkling champagne as we know it today wasn't really 'invented'; it was a result of Champagne's cool climate and its effect on the wine's chemistry in the cellar. In cold winters the chill would stop the fermentation before it was completed and then recommence in the spring when the temperatures were sufficiently warm to reactivate the remaining yeasts and sugars in the wine. This secondary fermentation gave off carbon dioxide, which is what makes the bubbles, and was originally seen as an infuriating fault in the wine.

Dom Pérignon, a Benedictine monk making still wine here in the 17th century, referred to this unwanted fizz as *le vin du diable* ('the devil's wine'). What's more, the bottles were made from low-quality French glass and would frequently explode when the pressure within them became too great. One can only imagine the frustration, not to say potential injuries, when yet another bottle shattered into smithereens, discharging its sticky contents all over the cellar. I bet the good monk whispered filthy profanities under his breath as he reached for the mop and bucket once more.

Understandably, winemakers were eager to get rid of these bottles as soon as they could, so they'd pack them up and palm them off on whoever would take them. They sent them to the hapless British (the Anglo-French wine trade being well established by then), doubtless chuckling into their grubby habits. *Quelle surprise*! The Brits received them with unbridled joy, for they loved this novelty sparkling wine and would often re-bottle it when it arrived from France to increase its lifespan. They had some experience of such things – their own cider sometimes turned out fizzy – and had developed a method of making glass tough enough to withstand the pressure of bottle fermentation. They also used cork stoppers rather than wooden bungs wrapped in rags as were favoured by the *champenoise*. These two innovations were the key to keeping the wine intact, and often actually improving it as it aged.

Flamboyant, fun-loving Charles II adored this new-fangled wine, as frothy as his collars and cuffs – well, he would, wouldn't he? – and its popularity soared among the aristocracy and the aspirational. Dom Pérignon and other winemakers saw this gap in the market and hastily began experimenting with their winemaking techniques, using English bottles and cork stoppers.

'Come quickly! I am drinking the stars!' is the oft-quoted exclamation by Dom P as he called his monastic chums around him in the winery on 4 August 1693 to show he'd finally mastered the technique. This is probably nothing more than 19th-century marketing nonsense promulgated to, in modern parlance, raise brand awareness, but we do know that it was Dom Pérignon's sparkling wine that was used to toast the Duc D'Orléans when he became Regent of France in 1715 (he declared it 'basically wholesome, being so gentle and frothy'), and later when the young king Louis XV took the throne in 1723. That clinched it; new-age champagne was the future and other makers started muscling in, Nicolas **Ruinart** and Claude **Moët** being among the first to the party, with plenty of others joining in during the 19th century.

Champagne was being necked by the great and the good across the Continent and across the pond. Russian Tsar Peter the Great brought it to his decadent court, and later Empress Catherine the Great, she of the various voracious appetites, declared it the greatest aphrodisiac and used it to, erm, fortify her soldiers as well as her lovers. It did champagne's reputation no harm at all to be seen as the Viagra of the 18th century, a reputation that survives (rightly or wrongly) to this day.

The three main grapes of champagne are chardonnay, pinot meunier and pinot noir. *Blanc de blancs* on the label means it's 100 per cent chardonnay; *blanc de noirs* is made from either or both of the red-skinned pinots. If it doesn't say either of these on the label, it means it's a blend of all three. Pinot blanc, petit meslier and arbane grapes are allowed as well, but as together they make up less than 0.02 per cent of total plantings, they needn't concern us much here. Rosé champagne either (most usually) starts as white and is given its colour with the addition of a little red wine, usually made from pinot noir, or is left in contact with the red grapes after pressing to draw some colour from their skins.

Most of us are familiar with at least some of the *grand marques* champagne houses, many of which have been around for more than 150 years – **Krug, Bollinger, Veuve Clicquot, Taittinger** and the rest. These have become big brands, projecting their own values and the lifestyles with which they like to be associated with lavish advertising campaigns and trading. They all make reliable NV (non-vintage) champagne, blended so it always tastes the same, as well as vintage champagnes only in years when the grapes have been particularly good. They also produce special wines for special people, the costly prestige cuvées beloved of rappers, footballers, bankers and anybody else with the wherewithal to flash the large sums of cash required. Some, like good old

Dom Pérignon, only release vintage champagne and only in exceptional years, which partly explains its constant high price.

Most of us have our favourite of these when we want to be sure we know what we're getting – mine is **Pol Roger**'s Brut Reserve – but it's worth looking out for what are known as 'grower champagnes'. These are made by wine-makers who grow their own grapes and so see the process through from beginning to end. Big brands buy up grapes grown by many growers (some of whom make their own champagnes), and sometimes juice, from all over the region. These smaller growers take the best juice for themselves and sell their surplus to the big houses. Grower champagnes tend to offer wines of more interest and higher quality, wines that more clearly show the character of their particular terroir, and while they're never cheap, they tend to offer better value in the glass compared with the big brands.

CREMANTS

Crémant (meaning 'creamy') is the word canny shoppers look for to get more bubbles for their buck. Crémants are made in exactly the same way as champagne but come from other regions – Alsace, the Loire, Jura, Limoux, Bordeaux, Savoie and Burgundy (Bourgogne) – and are made with whatever grapes are allowed in their appellations, which may include those used in Champagne. They don't carry the same status as champagnes and thus don't command such high prices, but many make really terrific sparkles that cost around the same as far more inferior fizz.

The Limoux region in the Languedoc, by the way, lays rightful claim to be the first in France to make sparkling wine. Benedictine monks were making it in the abbey at Saint-Hilaire in 1531, nearly 200 years before the Champe-noise had nailed the technique. 'Blanquette de Limoux' is still made here with the local grape mauzac, along with some very good crémants.

PROSECCO

Those of us in the booze biz tend to be sniffy about cheap prosecco – sweet yet often acrid, with ruthless or weedy acidity and plenty other sins besides – but the stats show the civilians love it, so who are we to sniff?

It's less than a tenner a bottle, after all, and as we all know, a glass of fizz is about so much more than just what we taste. It's about joy and celebration, even if that's just a TFI Friday feeling (or even a TFI Tuesday-and-at-least-I'm-still-alive feeling), and more often than not we raise a glass of fizz and make a toast to something good. It should be an affordable pleasure for all and not something for only the wealthy or just for the most special of occasions.

Prosecco is the region around Treviso just north of Venice in Italy. The wine is made from the glera grape, originally from Slovenia, and although it has been made for more than a century, it was only in the early 1980s that it really took off. Prosecco is usually made by what's known as the charmat method, when the wine is refermented in pressurised stainless steel tanks then bottled, although some use the *metodo classico* (or *méthode traditionelle*, as the French would have it) when the secondary fermentation takes place in the bottle. The latter – used to make champagne – is considered to produce higher-quality wine.

To get to the best of prosecco, look for those from the two DOCGs (*Denominazione di Origine Controllata e Garantita*), the highest classification for Italian wines. It denotes controlled (*controllata*) production methods and guaranteed (*garantita*) wine quality found in only specified regions: fruity little numbers from Conegliano Valdobbiadene or the less commonly found Colli Asolani.

The Brits love prosecco so much they drink more than twice as much as do the Italians. Far from pissing off the traditional sparkling wine regions of Champagne and (somewhat less traditional) southern England, this incredible passion for prosecco has also amplified our thirst for other fizz and seen sales of these skyrocket.

FRANCIACORTA

Franciacorta is the posher cousin of prosecco, the one with the designer clothes and better jewellery, hailing from the hills of Lombardy around the fashion capital of Milan, always made by the *méthode traditionelle* from a combination of pinot noir, pinot meunier, chardonnay and pinot bianco (the grapes of champagne itself). Wine has been made here for centuries but it was only in 1961 that an ambitious winemaker at the Berlucchi estate tried his hand at something fizzy and this was the result. Franciacorta has stringent rules for those that bear its name and it produces very high-quality wine, the best of which stands shoulder high to decent champagne and comes with prices to match.

LAMBRUSCO

Yes, yes, I *know*. Lambrusco is, for many of us, remembered unfondly, like a misguided liaison that ended in tears. It was a sweet, fizzy red horror we flirted with briefly in our youth – it seemed quite avant-garde in the art-school 1980s (It was red! It was fizzy! It was cheap!) – but now we hang our heads in shame at the memory of being seduced by such dross.

Little did we know. What we were drinking was a travesty of the real lambrusco, which has been made in the Emilia-Romagna and Lombardy regions for centuries. Some claim the Romans' *lambrusca* wine (meaning it came from wild grapes growing on the edges of fields) was re-fermented in clay amphorae and left until it became fizzy, but let's not get distracted by history here.

Traditional lambrusco is made by the *metodo classico* or, sometimes, the *metodo ancestrale*, a tricky, hard-to-control technique whereby a secondary fermentation occurs in the bottle but without the addition of sugar to kickstart it, or the disgorging to remove sediment, as is done with the traditional method.

Lambrusco is the name of both the style of wine and the family of grapes from which it's made. Proper lambrusco is dark and full of brambly fruit but has an appetising dryness and makes a nicely leftfield aperitif, especially in the winter when one needs every iota of red wine-warmth one can get. Serve chilled, but not too cold; a spunky salami or slices of grainy parmesan make very good accompaniments.

ASTI SPUMANTE

This is another Italian sparkling wine that has had many crimes committed in its name but there are some good examples to be had. It's made around the towns of Asti and Alba in Piedmont, always from the moscatel grape. Fruity rather than sugary-sweetish, softly sparkling and at a very gentle 5.5%-or-so abv, asti spumante is traditionally drunk chilled as an aperitif, though it goes well with fruity puddings too.

Similar things are made in other places – the Australians are particularly good at them and often make them pale pink and very girly, sweetish and low in alcohol but fun enough for a summery kick-off, especially if you pop a strawberry or raspberry into the bottom of the glass.

BRACHETTO D'ACQUI

Brachetto is a red grape from Piedmont and is made into wine both still and sparkling. Fizzy brachetto d'acqui smells of strawberries and cream and, like its regional white relations from Asti, is slightly sweet and weighs in at a modest abv of around 5.5%.

FIZZ FROM OTHER PLACES

ENGLAND

At a famous tasting in London in 2015, a dozen demon wine pros judged a dozen sparkling wines, four from England, the rest from Champagne. The wines were tasted blind – the judges didn't know what they were tasting – and given marks out of 20. Somewhat astonishingly, the two top-scoring wines were English. *Sacré bleu*! **Hambledon** and **Nyetimber** beat Pol Roger, Taittinger and other *grand marque* champagnes, something that would have been unthinkable only five years previously. English sparkling wines have come a long way, helped by the rise in temperatures that climate change has brought, and those in the know think it's only a matter of time before they will be considered the best sparkling wines in the world.

The modern English wine industry can be traced back to 1951 when Major General Sir Guy Salisbury-Jones, on his retirement from the diplomatic service, was considering how he might best use the land around his house in Hambledon in Hampshire. He was a wine lover and noticed the similarities between the chalky soils around his house and those in the Champagne region. He consulted his friend Winston Churchill who introduced him to the chaps at Pol Roger, makers of his favourite champagne. Pol Roger sent their vineyard supervisor to oversee the first planting in 1952 and in 1955 Hambledon released England's first commercial table wine.

The winery went through several changes of ownership in the following decades and is now in the hands of Ian Kellett, who acquired the property in 1999 and replanted the vineyard with chardonnay, pinot meunier and pinot noir. He also revived the relationship with Pol Roger, who recommended **Duval Leroy**'s Hervé Jestin as *chef de cave* to direct the winemaking at Hambledon. Their first sparkling wine was released in 2014 (making wine is not for the impatient) and it is this that won the famed 2015 tasting.

There are now over 500 vineyards in England and Wales, the best producing sparkling wines of a quality that stands up favourably against those of Champagne. The strata of chalk that is found in Champagne dips below the English Channel and rises again in the rolling hills of Hampshire and parts of Sussex. This is why these areas produce sparkling wines that are most similar to their French cousins, but wineries in other regions make tip-top fizz as well.

SPAIN

Cava has had something of a bad rep largely because, just like prosecco, there's an awful lot of rubbish around – cheap but not necessarily cheerful. About 95 per cent of cava (the Catalan word for 'cave') is made in the Penedès region of

Catalonia, mostly from macabeo, xarello and parellada grapes, although chardonnay and pinot noir are permitted as well.

Made here since the late 19th century, cava is always made by the *méthode traditionnelle,* the same method used in Champagne whereby the wine undergoes secondary fermentation in the bottle to produce the bubbles. Cava has improved hugely in recent years as the best makers lavish care and attention on their winemaking and focus on quality rather than quantity, many choosing to dispense with the word 'cava' altogether on their labels. Look for *reserva,* which means it's been aged for at least 15 months on its lees, the same as non-vintage champagnes, or *gran reserva* which means it has had at least 30 months on the lees.

GERMANY AND AUSTRIA

Germany and Austria make their own versions of sparkling wine they call *sekt.* Like many cavas and proseccos, much of it is pretty uninteresting, made from cheap wine imported from France, Spain and Italy and given its bubbles by secondary fermentation in tanks, but there are good examples to be had – 'Deutscher Sekt' on the label means it's made from German wine; *traditionnelle flaschengärung* indicates its secondary fermentation occurs in the bottle. Sekts made with riesling can really thrill when well made, as can those made with Chardonnay and grapes from the pinot family – noir, blanc, gris or meunier.

AUSTRALIA AND NEW ZEALAND

Australia and New Zealand are also in on the act, making some good champagne-esque wines from their cool-climate regions – Tasmania makes some of the best I've tasted. The Australians are also keen on sparkling reds, with shiraz being a favourite grape to fizz. They tend to be beefier and sweeter than their European cousins so are best taken with a kind of roll-your-sleeves-up-and-bring-it-on approach. They are not the most elegant or subtle of aperitifs but can make a cracking start to a winter evening with some spicy salami and an open mind. They are also, incidentally, a smart match for chocolate.

SOUTH AFRICA is also upping its game when it comes to bubbles to rival some of the best from Europe, and it's worth keeping an eye on those from **SOUTH AMERICA** and the **USA** too.

SHERRY

I have never been gladder to have a fan, that hand-held device made from concertinaed paper or fabric that wafts the air around you with little effort but so much elegance. Somebody gave me one the last time I was in sherry country, where the sun reflects off the chalk-white buildings searing blind spots into your eyes. Miraculously, I'd remembered to pack it for this trip.

We pile out of a taxi into the chaotic throng. 'Come,' says our host. 'Follow me.' It is the *Feria de Abril*, a week-long festival on the outskirts of Seville; it feels like the whole of Andalusia has come to play. It's the end of the day but still fearfully hot, and my fan comes into its own. Such a simple yet effective thing: all the ladies have them and mine makes me feel almost part of the crowd.

Everybody, to a man, woman and niño, is dressed up to the *nueves*; many are up to *diez*. The ladies wear extravagant *trajes de gitano* – flamenco dresses fitting tight to the knee then splaying out in sensational ruffles, accessorised with tasselled shawls pinned at the cleavage and flowers in their upswept hair, or they're in devastatingly elegant horsewoman's gear – long skirts, boxy jackets and black felt hats with razor-sharp brims. The men look dashingly handsome in collarless coats, cummerbunds and tight britches tucked into long leather boots, and they doff their dapper hats as they pass.

Even the horses are in their finery, with flowers in their fetlocks and bells on their bridles. Feeling, apart from the fan, horribly underdressed, I climb aboard an open-topped carriage and join the parade along with countless others on foot, on horseback or in carriages like ours.

What started in 1847 as a horse-trading market where the young might meet suitable spouses now serves more as an excuse for the Sevillanos to dress up and carouse for six days straight. Over 1000 *casetas* – gaily striped tents adorned with bunting – line the streets of this temporary encampment which smells mostly of horses and candy floss and sweaty saddles, and it's in these that the serious partying happens.

There is music, of course, and lots of dancing – *flamenquito* groups play impassioned *sevillanas* (the local form of flamenco) as couples stamp on the wooden floors with much sexy swirling and clacking of castanets – and of course there is drinking. Manzanilla sherry, bone-dry and salty and tasting of sun, is served with salted almonds, plates of velvety jamon and slices of perspiring manchego. We eat, we drink and we talk and suddenly it's 9 p.m.

These guys have been at it for hours but there's no sign of drunken unruliness – the Spanish are masters at pacing themselves – and many of them will still be here at dawn. My appetite suitably whetted, I flutter my fan demurely and make my excuses. I have a date at the bar of the Hotel Alfonso XIII with a matador I met on the plane. *Olé.*

Sherry is ingrained in the culture here, and it's very much a regional thing. If you ask for a manzanilla in Madrid or Barcelona you're likely to be met by a bemused *Que?* or possibly some chamomile tea – *manzanilla* is the Spanish word for chamomile and it's thought the wine got its name from its distinctive nose of wild flowers such as this.

Made only in a small corner of southern Spain in the region around the city of Jerez, from which it gets its name, sherry comes in many delicious guises, ranging from razor-sharp, bone-dry aperitif styles to the velvet-thick stickies that are almost puddings in themselves, with all the wondrously complex and varied wines in between.

The Phoenicians established the port of Cadiz around 1100BC and planted vines in the surrounding region, which they named Xera. The Phoenicians were demon traders, as were the Greeks and Romans who followed, and wine was made here for the local market as well as for export. Much of it must have been pretty filthy by the time it reached its destination, exposed to the salty air and rough treatment on the ships at sea. The Romans boiled up crushed grapes and added it to wine to sweeten it, but it's unlikely the resulting drink would bear much resemblance to sherry as we know it today.

It was the Moors who really made their mark here, occupying the land from 711AD and establishing an astonishing civilisation whose traces are still very much in evidence in the architecture, food and music of the region. Wine, of course, was prohibited to Muslims but they were allowed to use it 'medicinally', and were quite happy to allow its production by the Christian and Jewish infidels living alongside them, and to benefit from its trade with non-Muslim countries. Most significantly, Moorish alchemists developed the art of distilling high-strength alcohol, which was used to fortify wine to preserve it during its long but lucrative voyages.

The city at the centre of this winemaking region was known as Seris, later called Jerez when it was reconquered by the Catholic Spanish in the 13th century. From here the wine was sent to the ports of Cadiz and Sanlúcar de Barrameda where it was loaded onto the ships of the *Conquistadores* as well as those of traders.

The English were their keenest customers. Trade with the Brits was well established by the 16th century but it probably started much earlier – there are records of Spanish wine being imported to England as early as 1340. Strong bonds were forged between sherry houses and their English shippers, who corrupted the name Jerez to 'sherry', and many of these relationships survive today. By the 18th century, demand for wine was growing all over northern Europe, particularly among the nautical powers of Britain and Holland who wanted wine that would survive long voyages. Wine producers and shippers worked together to develop a method of wine production and ageing that would satisfy these growing markets. The solera system evolved during this time; not only did it result in wines of consistently reliable stability and quality, it imparted the unique characteristics that still make sherry wines stand out from the rest.

In the mid-19th century nearly half the wine drunk in Britain was Spanish sherry but it fell out of favour as cheaper approximations appeared from other places labelled as 'sherry' but coming, most commonly, from Australia, Canada and South Africa. This put the wind up the makers of Jerez who pushed for legal definition of their special wines and were granted one of the earliest examples of Denomination of Origin status in 1932.

HOW IS SHERRY MADE?

The palomino grape is used for all the dry styles of sherry. The wine is fermented as normal, usually in stainless steel tanks, and then the magic begins. Wines destined to become fino or manzanilla (they are made identically; *manzanilla* is the term used for those made in Sanlúcar de Barrameda where the sea air lends it its characteristic salty twang) are fortified with grape spirit to around 15% then put to age in wooden barrels (called 'butts' in sherryland) in overground cellars known as bodegas. These vast buildings, many built in the 19th century, look like cathedrals and smell like heaven. There are tens of thousands of butts in row upon row, from each of which the winemaker will taste at regular intervals using a *venecia*, a small cylindrical cup on the end of a long and flexible handle. It's inserted into a corked hole in the top of the butt and withdrawn with a flourish, whereupon the sherry is poured into a tasting glass with bullseye accuracy.

The microclimate of the region produces the unique airborne yeasts that are the key to sherry, and the bodegas are where these yeasts thrive. The butts are filled to about four-fifths of their capacity, then they are laid horizontally and stacked in rows upon each other in the system called the solera. The yeast grows to form a crust – known as the *flor* – on the surface of the wine that protects it from oxidation and, as it feeds on the residual sugars in the wine, renders it bone dry.

The oldest wines are in the butts on the bottom row of the solera system, and the youngest on top. When bottling time comes, the wine to be bottled is taken from the bottom row of the solera, with no more than one-third of each butt being drawn off. The extracted wine is replaced with wine from the butts above this row, which is in turn replaced with wine from the butts above. The butts on the top layer are topped up with that year's new wine and so the system evolves. The average age of wines blended in sherry must be at least three years but in reality many are much older than this.

Finos and manzanillas are bottled while the *flor* is still alive and intact. Those destined to become amontillados or palo cortados are left in the barrel after the *flor* dies off, so exposing the ageing wine to oxygen which lends sultry notes of roasted nuts and spices, dried apricots and hot buttered toast. Olorosos are fortified to about 18% which prevents a *flor* developing so it ages by oxidation only, often for many years, and are characteristically complex with notes of polished furniture, caramel and raisins. Finos, manzanillas, amontillados, olorosos and palo cortados are all termed *vinos generosos*, dry wines with a maximum 5g of residual sugar per litre.

Pedro ximenez and moscato grapes are made into sweet wines known as *vinos dulces naturales*. The grapes are left to shrivel to raisins before they're pressed, so concentrating their sugars. They have the colour of mahogany and the taste of proper Christmas pudding, but they shouldn't concern us here, for only a savage or, perhaps, your granny, would drink sweet sherry as an aperitif. *Vinos generosos de licor* are *vinos generosos* blended with *vinos dulces naturales* to give varying degrees of sweetness and are labelled Pale Cream, Medium or Cream.

It should be noted that the pedro ximenez grape is made into dry sherry-style wines in the region of Montilla-Moriles, south of Cordoba and home to the hottest vineyards in Europe. Here they make wines in the same way as sherry but can't call them that because they aren't in the region – sherry may only be called sherry if it's made in the designated Jerez area, a triangle formed by the towns of Jerez de la Frontera, El Puerto de Santa Maria and Sanlúcar de Barrameda. Wine from Montilla-Moriles are known only by the style in which they're made – fino, amontillado, oloroso etc.

W. Somerset Maugham simply described sherry as 'the civilised drink', and I couldn't agree more. It is understated but classy, packing a relatively modest punch of alcohol with a complexity of flavour that makes it something to sip rather than glug. Raymond Postgate wrote in *The Plain Man's Guide to Wine*, 'Sherry is the best drink before a meal. It has no superior except, for grand occasions, a glass of cool and dry Champagne… Sherry is infinitely superior to cocktails, except for the one purpose of making people drunk. It takes much more sherry than it does cocktails to make a woman or man noisy and silly; most people will never on sherry reach the levels of foolishness to which a series of cocktails will carry them.' Not that sticking to sherry will necessarily keep you sober; its alcohol levels start at around 15% and can go up to 20% or more, so sip it slowly from small glasses if you don't want to get too silly.

My fridge is rarely without a half-bottle of fino and/or manzanilla. Their salty, astringent twang gets the digestive juices going; the smell of the sea often triggers subconscious childhood memories which alleviate stress and anxiety, which is perhaps why dry sherry always makes me happy (and only sometimes silly). I often have a small glass when I'm cooking (a slug of sherry in place of wine will add a certain charm to many a sauce or braise), sometimes but not always with some roasted almonds or even a humble salted crisp. If you're feeling fancier, have something fishy to hand – manzanilla with oysters is a match even more than the sum of its considerably delicious parts.

Amontillados and palo cortados have more weight and profundity and are totally delicious alone, but if you're feeling peckish try them with slivers of cheese or any cured meat.

MADEIRA

George, 1st Duke of Clarence, is said to have been drowned in a butt of malmsey wine in 1478 as a punishment for his treachery; frankly I can think of few nicer ways to go. Malmsey, also called malvasia, is one of four main noble grapes made into the unique wines of the volcanic island of Madeira. (It is more likely that the malmsey in which the Duke was drowned came from Cyprus rather than Madeira, malvasia being a grape that was grown, and still is, across a wide area of southern Europe, but that doesn't make for as good a story.)

Madeira rises steeply out of the Atlantic 350 miles west of Casablanca, buffeted by winds and frequently capped with a bonnet of cloud. Discovered by the Portuguese in 1419, the island became an important victualling stop for ships sailing between Europe and the Americas in the following centuries.

Wine made here was fortified with grape brandy to help preserve it on its journey across the ocean aboard these ships. It was soon discovered that something magical happened during the voyage – the wine was exposed to high temperatures as it sailed through the tropics, as well as oxidation as it began to evaporate through the porous wood of the barrels. Heat and air, usually the sworn enemies of wine, made madeira extraordinary. Its fame spread quickly on both sides of the Atlantic and by the 18th century it was so highly regarded it was used to toast the American Declaration of Independence. By this time, the madeira makers had developed a technique of heating the wine artificially on the island to mimic the effects of the long sea voyages, and left space at the top of the barrel to allow the wine to oxidise.

What makes this wine so special is its incredible longevity. Once bottled, it is completely stable and stays miraculously fresh. This is why whenever I'm asked what my desert island wine would be, the answer is always, always madeira. I'm fortunate to have drunk old madeiras going back as far as 1827 that are thrillingly complex and concentrated but still possess energy and verve that come from its characteristic high acidity. As Winston Churchill, a big fan of the wine and the island, said, drinking madeira is 'like drinking liquid history'.

Madeira is made into styles with varying degrees of sweetness. The 'noble' grapes are, from the driest to the sweetest, sercial, verdelho, boal and malvasia, with the rare-as-hen's-teeth terrantez and bastardo sitting somewhere in the middle. Terrantez, difficult to grow and harder to find, is perhaps the most highly esteemed amongst madeira geeks for its particularly citric complexity, while bastardo, known elsewhere in the wine world as Trousseau, is even thinner on the ground. Only five vintages of bastardo were made in the past 200 years, the most famous being 1927 and the most recent 1954. Once almost extinct, the maker Barbeito has been replanting this grape and now has its first vintage, a 2008, in barrel. We may well all be dead before it is bottled.

Until recently only wines made from these grapes were allowed to specify them on their labels, but newish regulation now allows for tinta negra to be name-checked as well. Tinta negra is the most widely planted grape on the island and accounts for some 85 per cent of the total. It is the most versatile and resistant of grapes and may be made into any style. Once seen as merely a workhorse grape, fit only for blending and cooking, tinta negra is now being championed by the likes of Barbeito and made into some very fine wines that stand shoulder-to-shoulder with the noble varieties.

Some wines may be blended and sold labelled merely by style (dry, medium dry, medium sweet or sweet) and the average age in the blend, three years being the minimum. Even relatively young wines may be blended with something quite ancient from the producer's stocks. They may be labelled with a specific varietal as long as it comprises at least 85% of the total. Those aged for five years in cask may be labelled *colheita* with the year of their harvest, but could well sit happily in barrel for far longer before being bottled and released.

Frasqueira wines are those that have been aged for at least 20 years in cask and then for two or more years in bottle. They are labelled simply with the dominant varietal and the year of their vintage, and are the wines that command top dollar.

Rainwater is a style, not a grape, so called (allegedly) because an unknown importer once left a shipment of uncorked casks out in torrential rain on the docks of Savannah in Georgia, USA. He sold them on nonetheless to unsuspecting customers who declared this lighter, fresher style very much to their taste; rainwater is still the most popular madeira style among Americans. Always medium-dry and usually made from tinta negra, it is such an approachable and well-priced aperitif, and is the drink I usually recommend to madeira virgins.

I could bang on about madeira for ever, but I won't. Suffice to say sercials, verdelhos and rainwaters all make very fine aperitifs served chilled in a small (but not too small) wine glass. If I had to choose a favourite, it would probably be verdelho – it has that extra bit of flesh on its body that makes it ravishingly good alone but also very versatile with pre-dinner food – I love it with smoked or raw fish, hard cheeses and ham.

Reliable madeira makers include **Blandy's** (the oldest), **Barbeito** (the youngest), **Justino's** (the largest) and **D'Oliveras** (holders of the largest stocks of very old wines).

PORT

A fortified wine made in Portugal's Douro Valley, port is best known as an after-dinner drink, classically to be drunk with cheese. It owes its existence to the military fracas between France and Britain in the early 18th century when French ports were blockaded so the Brits had to look to their European allies for their wine. The Portuguese fortified their red wines with brandy to prevent it spoiling on its journey, which they shipped from the coastal town of Oporto at the foot of the Douro Valley. So began a close relationship between port wine and the British that continues to this day.

Vintage ports are bottled no more than two years after they are made, and the best will keep and improve for years or even decades before they are drunk, while LBVs (Late Bottled Vintage) may stay in barrel for up to six years before bottling. Both have a dark-red density and sweetness that makes them most suitable for post-prandial supping but when it comes to aperitifs, my eye is on tawny and white ports.

Tawny ports are aged in small barrels so undergo a degree of oxidisation as some of the wine evaporates through the porous wood; this gives them their characteristic tawny colour from which they get their name. Wines are often blended as the years go by and are only bottled when they're deemed ready to drink. Tawny ports have a delicacy and freshness which I adore in an aperitif context, and they needn't be costly; I love it just slung over a little ice, or perhaps in a First of the Summer Wine (see page 132). Having said that, I've been fortunate enough to drink a rare and valuable tawny port from the year of my birth that demanded nothing more than a lovely glass and a sense of wonder that something made more than half a century ago still has such splendid vivacity and perky charm. If only one could say the same for oneself.

Tawny port was the traditional aperitif of the region for centuries until in 1934 Taylor's, one of the region's most famous makers, launched a port made from white grapes.

White port is now made by most port houses and is *the* aperitif of the region, either drunk on its own or, more commonly, mixed with tonic; it's also rightly gained traction recently amongst switched-on drinkers who know a good aperitif when they see one.

GIN

Oh dear lord, where would we be without gin? The go-to hooch of choice for so many of us come the end of a long day when we're in need of an easy pick-up. It's Mother's Little Helper (also Mother's Ruin), but it also hits the spot for so many with no maternal angst at all. Ladies' Delight, Cuckold's Comfort, Daffy's Elixir and The Cure for the Blue Devils: gin has been known by all these names and plenty more.

Gin has its roots in Holland's *genever*, coming from *gineverbes*, the Dutch word for juniper. Juniper is indigenous to the Low Countries; Flemish writer Jacob van Maerlant refers to a medicine made from juniper berries boiled in malted wine in his 1270 tome *Der Naturen Bloom* (The Flowers of Nature) and it seems its production increased widely after that. Juniper was used not only for its medicinal properties as an antiseptic and diuretic, it was also used to mask the taste of the highly alcoholic and grubbily distilled wine. By the 16th century tinctures made with juniper were being sold as medical remedies all over the country; by the early 1600s tax was being levied on genever and other alcoholic liquor, suggesting it had come out of the medicine cabinet and was being enjoyed as a recreational drink by then.

The Dutch were a nation of explorers, through which they came across ever-more exotic spices and other botanicals, which they began to add to their genever. It was taken on board the ships to kill the pain, if not the cause, of the tropical diseases they were bound to encounter and traded at the ports they visited along the way.

They were certainly trading *genever* with the English from the 1570s, and English troops fighting for the Dutch in the Eighty Years' War (1568–1648) developed a real taste for it, doubtless for its power to give what became known as 'Dutch Courage' in the face of fear and fatigue on the battlefields, as well as for its soothing qualities in times of downtime drinking. They brought it back with them and shared it with their friends.

Gin then caught on big time, certainly among the lower orders, and the English were soon making it for themselves. Our binge-drinking Brexit Britain began here, it seems. 'The English, who hitherto had, of all the northern nations, shown themselves the least addicted to immoderate drinking, and been commended for their sobriety, first learn'd, in these Netherland wars, to swallow a large quantity of intoxicating liquor, and to destroy their own health by drinking that of others,' reported snooty historian William Camden (1551–1623), and even the normally liberal playwright Thomas Nash noted somewhat priggishly that 'Superfluietie in drink' was 'a sinne, that ever since we have mixt ourselves with the Low-countries, is counted honourable.'

Polite society in Britain favoured French brandy over this newfangled gin but after William of Orange came from Holland to become king of England in 1689 and brought his *genever* habit with him, it was suddenly deemed mannerly amongst the elite as well to drink whatever 'Dutch Billy' was having. Fashion is, and always will be, such a very fickle thing.

King Billy slapped a ban on the import of all foreign spirits in 1690 which led to a massive increase in domestic production of gin in the UK, both legal and illegal. Most of this would have tasted so revolting it had to be sweetened with sugar as well as any other 'botanicals' they had to hand, whether or not juniper was involved; turpentine and sulphuric acid were also common additions. For reasons we don't really have time to go into here (but yes, cats were involved), this became known as Old Tom. Distillation and licensing laws were slackened to keep up with demand; 70 million litres (15 million gallons) of the stuff were legally distilled in 1743 for a population of just six million (30 million litres of gin were sold in the UK in 2016 to a population of 65 million), and it's estimated at least that much again was being brewed up illegally, often in people's bathtubs. Not only would that have put the nation's livers in jeopardy, it can't have done much for its standards of personal hygiene.

By the mid-18th century, London was in the grips of a gin craze and it was getting out of hand. Gin was the drink of the poor; it was cheaper than beer and safer than water, and its sweetness and alcoholic content would have helped ease the pangs of hunger as well as those of misery. Drunkenness reached epidemic proportions and with it came social breakdown as so famously recorded in Hogarth's 1751 'Gin Lane' etching, a shocking document of gin-crazed Londoners going to moral and physical rack and ruin. Something simply had to be done and the government, seeing drunkenness as the cause of poverty and not the other way round, that same year passed the Gin Act, clamping down on illegal distilleries and substantially raising taxes on the production and sale of gin. Prices shot up and distilleries shut down, and rising grain costs after a series of bad harvests meant prices rose still further. This, together with the closure of many seedy drinking dens and gin shops, saw consumption finally slow down among the poor.

In 1761 Thomas Dakin established England's first commercial gin distillery at Warrington in the industrial heartland of Lancashire, where manufacturing machinery was at its most cutting edge. Gin was getting modern and, most importantly, it was getting clean. Dakin eventually sold his business to the Greenall brewing family and **Greenall's**, although now owned by Diageo, still makes gin to the same recipe at the same distillery, the oldest in the land.

Mention should also be made of a Scottish whisky maker who moved to London and began making gin in Southwark in 1769, using only the finest grains and botanicals available and distilling it three times for purity. Thank you, Mr Alexander Gordon. London dry gin was born, and **Gordon's** gin remains the same today, sneered at by many but with a place in my heart if it's export strength and I've got time to pick a bottle up at duty free without missing my plane.

London dry gin evolved further in the 19th century with the introduction of the column stills that made the distillation process more refined, so doing away with the need to add sugar to mask dubious ingredients. It is the classic juniper-led style most of us depend on – **Beefeater, Tanqueray** and **Berry Bros & Rudd No 3** are among the best – although Raymond Postgate, ardent communist and gourmet, in his 1951 *The Plain Man's Guide to Wine*, somewhat rudely described it as smelling 'like a rather vulgar woman's perfume.' Only natural botanicals may be used in London dry these days, though somewhat confusingly it doesn't have to be made in London.

This new style of gin was deemed clean and free from impurities and so appealed to those with an interest in the 'healthy' and 'refined' ways of doing things. The Victorians' sense of propriety and tendency to show off brought the rise of the gin palace in the mid-19th century. Extravagantly decorated with gilt-framed mirrors, brass rails and ornate mouldings, these temples to drinking sold gin from large barrels, often served with cakes or biscuits, and were far more glamorous than the tawdry beer houses frequented by the masses. Gin became seen as something for the sophisticated; the temperance and teetotal movements that shunned the demon drink saw levels of drinking fall further among the working classes and those that did partake tended to choose beer over gin because by then it was cheaper. Women, needless to say, were expected to stay at home sober while their men were at the pub.

Gin was the drink of the Empire, of course, swigged down with tonic water spiked with anti-malarial quinine – 'Gin and tonic has saved more Englishmen's lives, and minds, than all the doctors in the Empire,' Winston Churchill is supposed to have said – and when the American craze for cocktails reached this side of the pond (Charles Dickens was one of the first to write about them following a visit to Boston in 1842), gin really got into its stride. New York bartender and general boozehound Jerry Thomas published his *Bar-Tender's Guide* in 1862, in which he gives 24 recipes for gin-based cocktails, though it should be noted that the gin he was using would have been very different from what we know today.

The Jazz Age fops and flappers drank gin with sybaritic abandon but it was also so frequently referenced in much of the popular culture of the time it found its way into the heart of the ordinary drinking classes. Somerset Maugham, F. Scott Fitzgerald, Raymond Chandler, Ernest Hemingway, George Orwell, Evelyn Waugh and so many more were all gin-drinkers and so were many of their characters, both the glamorous and the down-and-out.

The Queen, her mother and her sister drank gin and so did their loyal subjects at home and in pubs across the land. In the latter half of the 20th century it was required by etiquette to have bottles, or preferably decanters, of gin and whisky on the sideboard in every middle-class home, possibly along with some sherry. Gin is democratic and it's also pretty gender-neutral. Now, as it's been for decades, Colonel Blazer is just as likely to have a G&T at the golf club as is his good lady wife, whereas whisky (until very recently) has always been seen as a drink strictly for the boys. Gin is drunk by so many of us, from crusty old farts in Brexitland to the millennials moving on from alcopops and Jagerbombs; male, female, rich, poor, the lowly born and royalty.

Now we're in the grips of another gin craze, this one feeding on our seemingly insatiable appetite not just for quantities of any old gin; this time we want the NEW. You want gin flavoured with asparagus, green tea, seaweed or saffron? Or perhaps you'd prefer coconut, cocoa nibs or maybe a touch of lavender? They're all out there waiting for you to try, should the mood take you. My personal feeling on lavender as a flavour is that it only belongs in old ladies' knicker drawers, but *chacun à son goût*. Peanut butter gin? It's surely only a matter of time.

There are hundreds of gins out there, the good, the bad and the frankly ugly. The current Guinness World Record holder for the bar with the most gins behind it is found, somewhat incongruously, not in a swanky gaff in London or New York but in a pub, the Old Bell Inn in Oldham on the edge of the Yorkshire Moors, which has held this title since 2014 and stocks over 900.

This new gin craze is barely a decade old but, boy, has it come a long way. Following a relaxation of laws granting licences to distill spirits, **Chase Distillery** in Herefordshire launched in 2008, closely followed by **Sipsmith** in London in 2009. At that time there was only a handful of distillers around the UK; by 2017 that number stood at 273 with new gins appearing almost weekly.

Purists would say a gin should be made from scratch in a distillery, taking mash from the fermented raw ingredient – usually grains, sometimes potatoes, occasionally apples, though in theory anything containing starch will do – then distilling it with botanicals (juniper must be the dominant flavour) to a strength of around 96% abv, which is then let down with water to a more manageable 40% or thereabouts.

Most of the new gins today are made from industrially produced neutral grain spirit which is then re-distilled, or simply infused, with botanicals (artificial juniper flavouring is allowed, it should be noted).

While I wonder what the point is of messing around with gin so much it tastes like suncream or a bar of soap, I defend to the end the right of people to make and drink the stuff. Some of these wackily flavoured gins I've enjoyed for their novelty, but when it to comes to something to have in my store cupboard,

I'm a traditionalist and go for something with a clean streak of juniper coming through the background botanicals.

Nearly all the professional bartenders and boozehounds I know name **Beefeater London Dry** as their preferred gin, not just for a textbook G&T but as a cocktail ingredient that asserts itself clearly but doesn't muscle in too much on other ingredients. If you want something super-charged with juniper, try **Hepple** from Northumbria.

Old Tom is a style that's being revived, sweetened like in the old days and often flavoured with liquorice, and appealing to those who find juniper-heavy gins too bitter – **Jensen's**, **Hayman's** and **Bathtub** are just some of the fine examples around.

Plymouth is another style, less dry and more earthy than London gin. It may only be made in the city of Plymouth and currently there is only one surviving maker, the eponymous **Plymouth Gin Distillery**, established in 1793 when the city was a major port for the British Navy. Their cardamom-heavy 'Navy Strength' gin, bottled at 57%, was understandably popular among the sailors when they thirstily came ashore, and is still available, along with their more moderate and very good 41.2% Original Plymouth Gin.

Navy Strength gin gets its name from the days in the 18th century when pursers (then known as 'pussers') on British ships would test the strength of the gin to be taken on board to check it hadn't been watered down. The gin would be mixed with a little gunpowder and then heated by concentrating the rays of the sun through a magnifying glass. If the mixture ignited, it was deemed to be of sufficiently high strength for the seamen and was termed 'proof'; if it was so strong that it went off with a bang it was known as 'overproof'.

Hendrick's, with its rose and cucumber notes, is perhaps the most famous of what are known as 'New Western' or 'International Style' gins, those where the juniper notes are overshadowed by other flavourings; **Gin Mare** is another enjoying global success, playing on savoury Mediterranean notes of olives, rosemary and thyme. Much is made of 'locally foraged' ingredients in many of these new-age gins, along with words such as 'artisanal' and 'hand-crafted' slipped into their marketing. Many of them are very good but space restrictions prevent me from mentioning them all here. Some, however, are horrid.

This current gin craze astonishes so many of us in the booze business. We were all saying at least five years ago that the gin boom was getting ridiculous and surely it had reached its peak. Yet it shows no signs of slowing down, and we continue to be amazed at the drinking world's seemingly insatiable appetite for gin, which just goes to show how little we supposed 'experts' know.

VODKA

For many of us vodka is the spirit with which we first became acquainted. Having virtually no flavour it can be mixed with anything without really interfering, delivering only the required hit of alcohol with none of those nasty flavours found in grown-up drinks.

When I was young, vodka mixed with cranberry juice was the default drink for me and my friends in the restaurant world. Somebody had told us cranberry juice was so incredibly health-giving it virtually cancelled out the damage from booze, and it cured cystitis to boot. Sometimes we'd add a bit of grapefruit juice to make a Sea Breeze – the extra vitamin C added extra virtue, you see – and when we were feeling sophisticated and 'to-hell-with-healthy cranberry' we'd have a vodka and tonic. We weren't set up as a cocktail bar so these were easy drinks to put together and would happily see us through a long night of after-hours partying. 'Vodka's really clean,' we'd say. 'It's the smoking that gives me the hangover.' I also have it on good authority that expensive vodka (**Belvedere** or **Grey Goose**) and tonics are on the after-show debauchery rider of some of our nation's finest rock stars because 'it's really pure, man' and doesn't make them hungover. These guys really know how to party so they may well have a point.

This perceived 'purity' is the cornerstone of modern vodka marketing. Much is made of 'selected', often 'organic' grains; water that comes from Swedish glaciers, Canadian icebergs, Himalayan snow or mystical underground springs; multiple distillations and/or filtrations through charcoal, micron paper, quartz crystal, ground-up diamonds and even gold. The more arcane the better, and the more expensive too, particularly if they are 'limited editions' and come in a fur-lined gift box. These super-premium vodkas are made for the kind of vulgarian who thinks spanking five grand on a bottle of vodka makes them big and clever because, like, it's got actual 22-carat edible gold leaf in it AND it comes with a tacky diamond-encrusted gold pendant dangling from its neck, presumably to give to the long-legged hooker sitting on his lap.

The lack of botanicals and other additives in good vodka does indeed make it marginally less likely than other spirits to lead to a stonking hangover, but let us not forget the primary cause of a hangover is dehydration. Ask anybody who has sat down in Moscow with a group of unreconstructed bear-sized Russians and given uncountable shots of neat vodka over a pork-heavy dinner with no water on the side. Darling, I nearly died.

The Russians and Poles bicker over who invented vodka. The first documented production of vodka in Russia appears at the end of the 9th century, while the Poles lay claim that their *woda* was being made a century earlier.

As we can only trace the process of distilling as we know it to Arabian alchemists somewhere around the 10th century, heaven only knows how these drinks were made, but we do know that a British envoy to Moscow described vodka as Russia's national drink in the 14th century and it was known as that of Poland by the 16th century.

The word 'vodka' (a diminutive form of *voda*, the proto-Slavic word for water) first appeared in documents from the Polish court in 1405, though at this time is was mainly taken as a medicine, while the term *gorzałka* (meaning 'to burn') was given to the drink itself. The pot still was introduced in Russia in the mid-15th century and vodka was soon being produced in large quantities; the first exports, to Sweden, being recorded in 1505, and by then the production of Polish vodka as a drink and not a drug was also in full swing. Polish physician Stefan Falimierz claimed it would 'increase fertility and awaken lust' in his 1534 book on herbs, which may go some way to explain its popularity.

Production techniques were pretty rudimentary back then. Grains or potatoes were fermented then the resulting low-strength alcohol was distilled, the distillation process having to be repeated several times to rid the vodka of impurities. Much of this would still have been pretty undrinkable so fruits and/or botanicals were often added to take the edge off the burn. The Polish brand **Zubrówka**, distilled from rye and flavoured with its distinctive blade of bison grass, dates from this time and it's still around today.

Industrial production of commercial vodka in both Russia and Poland kicked off big time in the late 18th century following the invention in St Petersburg of a continuous distillation process with a charcoal filter system that finally made vodka clean and palatable and, most importantly, affordable to almost all.

We know that vodka was virtually unheard of in the rest of Europe and America until the end of the 19th century when travelling wine merchant Maurice Meyer began importing it into England from Poland to meet the demand of refugees from the Russian and Polish pogroms, but it failed to pique the interest of English natives until much later.

Pyotr Arsenyevich Smirnov set up his eponymous distillery in Moscow in 1862. By 1886 his vodka was granted a royal seal of approval and Smirnov was eventually awarded the Order of St Vladimir, making him and his descendants members of the aristocracy. They became fabulously wealthy as sales soared to a million bottles a day at the start of the 20th century; in 1911, 89 per cent of all alcohol drunk in Russia was vodka.

Then came the Russian Revolution of 1917 and everything changed. Vodka distilleries were taken under state control and Smirnov's son Vladimir was forced to flee, leaving his wife and children behind, first to Poland and then to Paris where he set up a small distillery and changed its name to Smirnoff. Vlad was not as good a businessman as his father had been and in 1934 he sold his failing company to Rudolf Kunett, a Russian-born American (whose family coincidentally had supplied the Smirnovs with much of their grain back in Russia) who started a **Smirnoff** distillery in Connecticut. It was not a success. The Americans were slow to catch onto the charms of this 'white whiskey'; they didn't take to the traditional way of drinking vodka, knocked back from small glasses in shots, and the faltering brand was sold to John Martin, chairman of liquor company Heublein in 1939. Other members of the company's board were not impressed as sales continued to stagnate.

Desperate to find a market for Smirnoff, Martin took to the road. The story goes that he was drowning his sorrows in the Cock 'n' Bull tavern on Hollywood's Sunset Strip some time in the early 1940s. Jack Morgan, the bartender, commiserated – he'd developed a house brand of ginger beer that had failed to excite his customers and was lumbered with quantities of unsold stock. Another customer present butted in to say he felt their pain – he'd inherited a company making copper mugs which he was finding impossible to shift. In a fit of inventive (and possibly drunken) genius the Moscow Mule was born – vodka mixed with ginger beer and served in the copper mugs which were engraved with the Smirnoff crest and the name Moscow Mule.

Buoyed by his success Martin set off on a marketing journey of some brilliance. He bought one of the first Polaroid cameras and travelled from bar to bar armed with the vodka, the ginger beer, the mugs and the camera. He'd asked bartenders to pose twice with a mug of Moscow Mule and a bottle of Smirnoff then he'd leave one photograph as a souvenir and take the other to the next bar to show its competitors what they were missing. Between 1947 and 1950 sales of Smirnoff tripled, and nearly doubled again in 1951 and despite (or maybe because of) anti-Russian sentiment during McCarthyism of the 1950s, vodka finally took off not just in the Moscow Mule but as a new ingredient for the cocktail bar.

Vodka in general, and Smirnoff in particular, really hit the global jackpot and became the drink of glamour and aspiration when it appeared in *Dr No*, the first James Bond film, in 1962. In Fleming's original 1958 novel, Bond specifies 'a medium Vodka dry Martini – with a slice of lemon peel. Shaken and not stirred please. I would prefer Russian or Polish vodka.' In the movie, Sean Connery's Bond just specifies 'vodka'. Bottles of Smirnoff Red appear prominently in this and subsequent Bond films – an early example of product placement and one that still endures.

Smirnoff cemented its reputation in the States through a series of high-profile ads in the 1960s featuring big stars of the day: Groucho Marx revealing two bottles of vodka secreted in the lining of his coat with the strapline 'If they don't serve Smirnoff, bring your own,' and a diamond-clad Zsa Zsa Gabor purring: 'If you like rocks, darling, try 'em with Smirnoff.' Smirnoff remains the world's bestselling vodka, closely followed by Sweden's **Absolut Blue**. It's odd to me how these two brands really divide professional drinkers of my acquaintance; some swear by one and despise the other, others hate or rate them both. I'm quite happy with either if I'm mixing them into a long drink, but would be more discerning where I to be contemplating something short where the vodka takes centrestage.

'In Russia they don't only drink to get drunk, they drink to stay drunk too, and no wonder,' as Kingsley Amis wryly noted. He suggests mixing equal quantities of vodka and rough red wine over some ice and stir in some 'sticky liqueur' as something to 'add interest to even the lousiest leg of the World Cup'. I've tried it using Triple Sec and can almost see his point, though I am not a football fan so it would take something with more fireworks to keep me involved till the final whistle.

As for vodka as an aperitif, sipping neat vodka is something of a thing with serious drinkers, either straight from the freezer as a shot, or perhaps in a tumbler with just a little ice. The former is the traditional Slavic way of doing things, ideally accompanied with caviar or an oily sliver of smoked fish. It's not a habit I indulge in often, though I can see that in good vodka there may be enough subtle nuances of flavour and texture to hold one's interest, and on the one occasion in my life I've had proper caviar with frozen vodka (Grey Goose, since you ask; caviar suits wheat-based vodkas), I have to admit it gave me a tingle of pleasure that made me blush. Decent smoked salmon with **Russian Standard** or **Reyka** Icelandic vodka straight from the freezer is a poor girl's alternative with a similarly sexy hit.

If I were having a Vodka Martini before dinner I'd certainly go for something a little bit smart on the vodka front, and I'd ask for it to be made on the dry side (i.e. holding back on the vermouth) to give the vodka a chance to shine through. I like the caraway-scented savouriness of rye-based Polish vodkas such as **Wyborowa**, although I'm also partial to the full-bodied richness of the parvenu **Tito's** vodka, created by the improbably named Tito Beveridge II in Texas. Noilly Prat would be my preferred vermouth, mixed at no more than 1:12 with the vodka.

When it comes to mixing vodka with other things, I defy anyone to tell the difference between Smirnoff and any of the higher-end vodkas when mixed in a vodka and tonic, and most definitely in a Bloody Mary; I certainly can't. The the only reason I'd have **Stolichnaya** instead (first made in Russia in 1938 and launched into the West in 1953) is because it's got a better label. Avoid the very cheapest of the cheap as they often have a paint-thinner burn that can rasp a bit even with the cunning cloak of a mixer.

BITTERS

Bitters in this context differ from the Italian generic 'amari' in that they are made for seasoning rather than drinking. They're very concentrated and very bitter, so a few drops are all you need to give a lift to so many drinks. **Angostura** is the classic (so familiar yet still exotic, with its sexily scented woody notes) with **Peychaud's** (almonds with a whisper of anise) not far behind. **Fee Brothers** do a great range of more outré flavours, and there are several other newer makers doing the same – **The Bitter Truth** and the **Australian Bitters Company** are worth looking out for.

Take your pick (or picks) and play around with them as you please to add a *je ne sais quoi* to whatever you're drinking. I'm most partial to orange bitters and use it to add an extra dimension to so many aperitifs (it's brilliant with Campari) and grapefruit bitters is also always close to hand. Bitters made with warm spices such as cloves or cinnamon give an extra thwack of flavour to anything involving red vermouth.

On days when I'm not drinking (and yes, there are a few) I often add bitters to tonic water with plenty of ice to deliver just enough underlying bitterness to make it feel like a 'proper' drink. It should be noted that all bitters are alcoholic, some as high as 45% abv or more, but they are used in such small quantities they are unlikely to bother a breathalyser.

ANGOSTURA

Angostura bitters were created in 1824 by Johann Siegert, a German doctor serving in Simón Bolívar's liberation army in Venezuela, in the town of Angostura. Originally made to combat the many digestive disorders suffered by the troops, Angostura became so popular Siegert began making it commercially and his sons continued the business, moving the production to the rather more politically stable island of Trinidad in 1875. Angostura is found on almost every bar around the world that is worth its salt. Despite its hefty 45% abv, Angostura bitters escaped the prohibition ban in the USA because it was deemed simply too bitter to drink alone, so came under the handy classification of being a medicine, which goes some way to explain why it finds its way into many classic cocktails. Its paper label that's rather too big for its bottle was allegedly an original manufacturing error that was left to become its now very distinctive branding.

Adding a few dashes of Angostura to a gin and tonic in place of a citrus garnish is very retro, perhaps harking from the days when lemons, let alone limes, were in short supply. So retro, in fact, it seems yet to appear on the hipsters' radar; try it.

ANISE-BASED APERITIFS

PASTIS

I am perched on a stool in a bar tucked down an alley near the harbour in Marseille, dressed in immaculately fitting capri pants and a crisp white shirt, a jaunty scarf tied at my long and elegant neck. It is the end of a hot summer day, and the air is warm and scented by the sea, the drains and the fishing nets piled on the nearby quay.

The moustachioed barman, gruff but with a gentle twinkle in his rheumy eyes, knows my name and what I like to drink. He presents me with the wherewithal: a tall glass with a generous slug of Ricard 45, a carafe of very cold water and a small bowl of ice. He offers me an untipped Gauloises which I accept demurely then place between my perfectly painted red lips and light with the proffered flame.

As I pour the water into the glass, the magic happens – the pastis turns from a clear, honey-hued shot of potential to an ethereal milky white, as if a cloud of the very smoke that curls seductively through the air has somehow been made liquid.

The door opens and a matelot strolls in – striped top, nifty cap, ruggedly unshaven and with the look of a man who's been at sea too long.

'*A l'eau; c'est l'heure*,' I say. Which, so deliciously, is the motto of the French Navy. Say it out loud and then you'll get it.

The sailor sits beside me and orders *un pastaga*, the local slang for pastis. He hangs his handsome head in his hands and mutters, '*Je suis dans le pastis*,' roughly translated as 'I'm in deep trouble.' And so the night begins…

Aniseed and its various relations are found in spirits distilled around the Middle East and the shores of the Mediterranean. The Greeks have ouzo, the Turks raki, the Macedonians make mastika, it's anesone in Italy and arak in Syria and Lebanon. Pastis is its French incarnation.

Whenever I drink this incredibly appetising aperitif, the rousing strains of *La Marseillaise* are never far from my mind. Along with coq au vin, Edith Piaf, the Eiffel Tower and berets, pastis is one of the great symbols of France. It has its roots in its bonkers older cousin, absinthe, first distilled in 1792 by one Pierre Ordinaire, a French doctor living in Switzerland, using aniseed as its flavour base and wormwood for its supposed hallucinogenic hit.

When absinthe was banned in 1915 for allegedly making half the nation mad, a gap was left in the aniseed-flavoured spirit market. Paul **Ricard** stepped into it with his eponymously named drink made *sans* the offending wormwood, which he launched in Marseille in 1932.

Ricard used Chinese star anise along with liquorice, fennel and other herbs grown on the sunny hills of Provence, and sweetened it with a little sugar. The **Pernod** clan, which was also making absinthe by then, soon followed suit, although they eschewed the use of liquorice, and pastis, or simply 'anis', became the favoured aperitif across the country.

What makes all anise-based drinks unique is that when water is added to the clear, yellowish liquid the drink becomes a milky-white, or *louche* as the French so fittingly call it. Aniseed contains oils called anetholes which are soluble in alcohol but precipitate out once the alcohol is diluted with water so rendering the drink cloudy.

The purist's way to drink pastis is to pour it into a glass, add four or five parts of cold water then, and only then, add ice. If ice is added to the pastis before the water, the anetholes precipitate out as crystals which float as a scum on top of the drink. I've experimented (a lot) and it seems to me that the scum appears anyway, whenever the ice is added, but it's certainly not unpleasant and has little impact on the enjoyment of the drink itself.

The Americans are said to drink pastis with Coca-Cola, what the French call a *mazout*. Reader, I tried it so you don't have to; suffice to say we should draw a veil over this act of wanton savagery and move swiftly on.

A sailor friend of mine takes pastis on all his voyages – he claims it makes a fine sundowner even in the absence of ice and, having put this to the test on a particularly choppy and chilly passage across the Bay of Biscay, I'd agree. These days I wouldn't be seen dead in a tent but I'd recommend pastis for keeping body and soul apart on cold and wet camping trips too. See also Whiskey Soda (page 144), for the same reason.

Ricard 45 always does it for me, but if I spot the **Janot** or (even better) Henri Bourdain brands I'd reach for them first. Mention should always be made of Tarquin's from Cornwall in the UK who make great Cornish pastis (geddit?), otherwise known as 'Kernow Pernod'.

ABSINTHE

Henri-Louis Pernod made the first French anise-flavoured spirit in 1805. Monsieur Pernod used aniseed to flavour his highly alcoholic spirit, along with wormwood, so called because it was said to cure intestinal worms, another common ailment of the time.

Pernod originally distilled his absinthe from wine but when vineyards across the country were devastated by the phylloxera outbreak in the 1850s – a mite that eats away at the roots of vines – he started using fermented sugar beet as the base for his hooch.

Deprived of their wine, the French embraced absinthe enthusiastically, not least because another of wormwood's active ingredients is thujone, a hallucinogen similar to the tetrahydrocannabinol (THC) found in marijuana. Absinthe fever swept the country, particularly among *le demi-monde* – the artists, writers, flâneurs and their floozies – who sought solace as well as inspiration from the potent drink, sometimes spiralling into madness. Oscar Wilde described drinking absinthe thus: 'The first stage is like ordinary drinking, the second when you begin to see monstrous and cruel things, but if you can persevere you will enter in upon the third stage where you see things that you want to see, wonderful, curious things.' Or, as Johnny Depp is said to have said, 'If you drink too much absinthe, you suddenly realise why van Gogh cut his ear off.'

In those days absinthe was made with about 260 parts per million of thujone; today it contains around 10 parts per million, but as many absinthes contain almost thermo-nuclear levels of alcohol – **La Fee's Parisienne** Absinthe socks a scary 68% abv – they should still be treated with wariness.

Absinthe is not really a drink to serve to people you don't know very well – its traditional preparation is rather arcane, involving dropping water from a decorative glass vessel fitted with a tap onto a sugar cube balanced on a flat filigreed spoon laid across the top of the glass. It is more fitting to a lost night with consenting adults than as something appetising before a meal with less depraved souls.

ARAK

Arak means 'sweat' in Arabic – more a nod to the way the spirit drips from the top of the still during the distilling process than to the possible effects of overindulgence – and is proudly declared as the national drink of Lebanon, that battered little country that continues to stand as a cosmopolitan, tolerant beacon in a region riddled with terrible strife. The best aniseed is said to come from Syria; the best arak makers in the Lebanon are eyeing their future stocks nervously.

Unlike pastis and many other anise-based drinks, arak is flavoured with nothing but aniseed, has no added sugar, and is generally bottled at a higher abv. Although the Lebanese makes some fantastic wine, arak is frequently drunk not only as a thirst-quenching aperitif but throughout the whole meal.

It's a drink to sip and consider slowly – its pungency is intense and quite overpowering to start, with initial sweetness on the nose and the palate giving way to something very savoury and astringent that makes you want to reach for the olives and pickled vegetables that are invariably served alongside to kick off any Lebanese meal.

The Lebanese mezze style of eating means many dishes are served together, and they generally burst with punchy and hugely contrasting flavours and textures. Grilled meat, fish and vegetables are big here, and arak's stridency stands up to their thwack of seductive smokiness. Spices and herbs often sing their own songs in dishes rather than just act as accents to other ingredients; such cacophonies would often drown out even the most well-meaning wine, but arak stands up well. It is curiously beguiling – its profoundly appetising, savoury layers settling onto the tip of the tongue ready to get along very nicely with whatever flavours come next. I would never dream of drinking pastis throughout a meal in France but somehow arak with a Lebanese feast feels very right.

OUZO

The Greeks' take on aniseed-flavoured hooch, probably named after the ancient Greek word *ózó* (smell). Traditionally drunk with iced water rather than ice, and always served with something to eat, ouzo is glorious with good black olives and feta cheese at the end of a day on the beach.

RAKI

Raki is a very similar thing in Turkey and the Balkans, and was indeed known as Turkey's national drink until 2013 when Prime Minister Recep Tayyip Erdoğan decreed that a yoghurt-based, alcohol-free drink called ayran had taken its place. Spoilsport. Often made with fruits such as figs and plums, as well as grapes, raki probably shares its roots with those of arak and ouzo, and is drunk in a similar fashion. Cheese is its most common companion, though I've heard of Turks drinking it with small green chillies dipped in Tabasco sauce to nibble on. I can't say this is a regular habit of mine, but it certainly clears the airways and gives that rather thrilling endorphin rush that comes with eating chillies, along with raki's muscular 40%-ish abv rating.

One last word on these very thrilling aperitifs, never store pastis or other anise-based drinks in the fridge. It makes them go cloudy and unattractive, which none of us wants to be. They're very strong and very easy to top up so should be approached with a wary eye but, boy, can they hit a certain hardcore aperitif spot with a bullseye.

AQUAVIT

Aquavit is the Nordic knockout spirit, made in the chilly climes of northern Europe, from Germany to as far as Finland, for centuries. The modish cuisine, novels, films and TV dramas from these countries has piqued the interest of stalwart booze boffins recently but aquavit is still pretty niche away from Scandinavian shores. Caraway and/or dill are the dominant and defining flavours, both being deemed as digestive aids, with dill, cumin, coriander, fennel, anise and cardamom being frequent bedfellows. In Sweden and Denmark it is usually distilled from wheat or rye and bottled straight from the still, while the Norwegians tend to favour potatoes as a base ingredient and age their aquavit in oak casks before bottling.

Aquavit – or *aqvavit*, or *akvavit*, or *akevitt*, depending on where you are – means 'water of life', and it comes under the general heading of 'schnapps', which covers the family of these strong drinks found across Scandinavian and Germanic countries. *Schnapps* means 'to gasp' or 'to bite it off' and refers to the proper way of drinking them, as a shot.

Greta Garbo was a great fan of aquavit, as befitted her Swedish roots. She famously hosted a Christmas party in Hollywood in 1930 at which she served a lavish 20-dish dinner including roast goose with all the trimmings and nothing to drink but aquavit, taken in the traditional manner. Nobody was allowed to leave until they'd stripped off completely and jumped into her swimming pool; one of the rare occasions she didn't want to be alone, one assumes, so she made the best of it.

Rather than a standalone aperitif, aquavit is usually taken with something to eat alongside – often smoked or salted fish or meat – then taken to the table to be drunk throughout the meal that follows. Beer rather than wine is usually offered as well, to keep thirst as well as extreme drunkenness from the door, although it should be noted that it is considered bad form to leave the table until the bottle of aquavit is empty.

There is still something quite formal, almost ritualistic, about drinking aquavit and it is still very much associated with celebration. Served very cold, ideally straight from the freezer or in a bucket of snow scraped from outside the log cabin, each shot is drunk as a toast to what seems appropriate at the time – births, deaths, friendship, the weather or whatever else seems a fitting excuse to lift the elbow. It is customary to look each other in the eye as one says '*skaal*' and knock it back in one. Singing often comes into the event as well, it being quite common for guests to bring along a song they've especially composed for the occasion.

I was once invited to an authentic Swedish *kräftskiva*, a traditional party to celebrate the crayfish harvest in late summer. There were crayfish, there was aquavit and there was singing (I dimly recall a song when we all had to pretend to be frogs) and yes, we did all end up in the pool. I felt for Greta Garbo's guests; I certainly wanted to be alone the next day.

To be honest, I hadn't drunk aquavit since then until I was researching this book. I'm happy to report that it has a rather outlandish appeal, especially in winter when nights set in early and seasonal gloom makes it seem somehow fitting. It's deeply savoury and very beguiling and has a lovely limpid turgidity when taken straight from the freezer. I like the Danish **Aalborg Taffel Akvavit** for its long and citrus-heavy finish, or **Linie** from Norway which undergoes a complex ageing process in old sherry or madeira butts that are sent to sea on a journey that specifically involves crossing the Equator twice. It is wonderfully deep and brooding, as one might expect.

Drink aquavit in shots if you're feeling brave and reckless, or in small tumblers if, like me, you'd prefer to sip to properly appreciate its profound allure. I like it with gravlax or pickled herrings served with dark rye bread and a resolution to stay away from the pool but, having said that, one of my life's ambitions is to drink aquavit after a sauna in the depths of a Nordic winter, preferably with the Northern Lights as a backdrop. One can but dream.

Aquavit is also good in a Negroni in place of the gin, or as a long drink with ginger beer or ginger ale; Nordic knitwear is optional.

5
THE RECIPES

1

GIN & TONIC

50ML/2OZ GIN
150ML/6OZ TONIC
SLICE OF LEMON, WEDGE OF LIME OR PERHAPS
A FINE STRIP OF CUCUMBER

THE VERY MAKING OF A G&T is an act to make the spirit soar. The clink-clink-clink of ice cubes tumbling into a spotless glass, the satisfying twist of opening the bottle then the glug-glug as the gin goes in. 'Psst' goes the tonic in an inviting manner when you open it, then the joyous bubbles cascade, tickling our noses when we get up close. Add an invigorating spritz of citrus and it's like liquid music in transparent form.

There is good reason that the gin and tonic could be said to be the apogee of aperitifs: not only is it a thing of great aesthetic beauty, it ticks all the physiological aperitif boxes as well. The alcohol in the gin cleans the tongue of lunch's debris while the underlying bitterness of its botanicals sets off alarm bells in our brains to get digestive juices flowing sharpish, and along with that comes the frisson of subconscious danger and its accompanying endorphin high. Tonic's quinine bitterness only intensifies the hit. Then come the bubbles – their tickling sensation on the tongue also encourages salivation – while the acidity of citrus makes it a hat trick.

There is a fashion, coming from the gin-loving Spaniards, to serve G&Ts in big, goldfish bowl-shaped glasses. They certainly can look impressive, but I have my reservations. Firstly, they're quite hard to hold. You end up clutching them with all your fingers and possibly some palm, which transfers heat and thus warms the drink. Plenty of ice is essential to mitigate such damage and you want it to last until you've reached the bottom of the glass, so we're talking serious volumes of ice here compared to that of liquid. In addition, the wide mouth of these goblets makes the bubbles of the tonic dissipate more

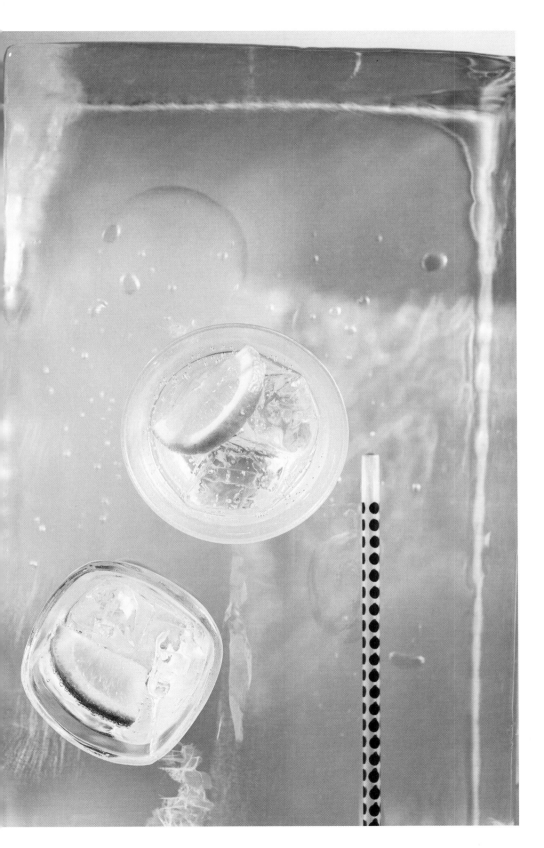

quickly, and the fizz is most definitely part of the fun. Also, the Spanish are far more generous when it comes to their measures – not for them the use of a jigger; they free-pour gin with gusto, unlike the uptight and law-abiding Brits whose G&Ts made in this fashion will almost certainly mean their miserly measures of gin will be beaten into submission by the quantities of ice and tonic used to make the drink look right.

In a bar I want the drink made in front of me, with the glass filled with ice first and the gin poured on top. I like to be asked what garnish I prefer – usually lemon, though lime is more modish, occasionally a twirl of cucumber skin. If the flesh of the citrus is rubbed around the rim before being dropped in the glass, so much the better.

My tonic should always be served in a small bottle or, even better, a can – never, ever those hateful guns – and I don't mind the bartender adding a little tonic to the glass then leaving the rest of the bottle alongside, but WOE BETIDE anybody who has the audacity to pour in the tonic up to the top of the glass. How very dare they assume they know how I like my dilution? It's very easy for the gin to be overpowered by the tonic; I like to taste it first as a one-to-one mixture then add extra tonic as I see fit.

And yes, I might (or might not) like a straw, perhaps two, instead of an irritating plastic stirrer that just gets in the way after it's done its job. (Having said that, I was once served a superlative G&T in George Clooney's suite in a smart hotel in the Italian alps. Tragically, George was not there at the time but the drink came with an exquisite stirrer, a long droplet of clear Murano glass that was an utter joy to use, first to stir the drink and then to lick before laying it down gently on the linen napkin. Reader, I stole it.)

The straw allows for gentle stirring and subsequent sipping, but a word of warning here: over-stirring will make the bubbles disperse quickly and flatten the tonic so use your straw and/or stirrer with caution.

At home I favour small cans of tonic (and yes, for me, it has to be Schweppes), over the larger individual bottles. These cans contain 150ml, which is just about right with a 50ml shot of gin. Large bottles of tonic just lose their fizz too quickly, and anyway seem flatter to start with than tonic from a can or small bottle. They may seem a cheaper option but unless you're serving six G&Ts at a time, they're generally a false economy.

2

MARTINI

**10 PARTS GIN
1 PART VERMOUTH
TWIST OF LEMON OR A GREEN OLIVE
TO GARNISH**

*Professional boozehounds agree to differ when it comes to their favoured
proportions of gin to vermouth, and when it comes to which brands they use.
This is my preferred recipe for a dry Martini, using 50ml No3 London Dry
gin and a teaspoon (5ml) of Noilly Prat vermouth. Fill a cocktail shaker or a
jug with ice then pour in the gin and the vermouth. Stir with a cocktail spoon
for no longer than ten seconds then strain into a chilled (very important)
cocktail glass. Garnish with a twist of lemon or a green olive. It should, as
one anonymous writer noted, resemble Fred Astaire in a glass.*

VARIATIONS

DIRTY MARTINI	Add a splash of olive brine, garnish with an olive
GIBSON	Garnish with a cocktail onion
PINK MARTINI	Add a splash of Angostura bitters
CHURCHILL MARTINI	No vermouth; simply stir the gin over the ice to chill and slightly dilute it and serve with an olive marinated in dry vermouth
DRIPPING (OR WET) MARTINI	Half-and-half gin and vermouth
BURNT MARTINI	Add a splash of a peaty whisky
BRADFORD	A shaken Martini (so called, rather unfairly to Bradford, that bluff town in Yorkshire, because it's always cloudy)
PARISIENNE	Add half a teaspoon of crème de cassis

THE AMERICAN WRITER H.L. MENCKEN claimed the Martini is 'the only American invention as perfect as the sonnet'. Quite a claim, but one that quite possibly stands up for the seasoned drinker, for a good Martini is an aperitif of great, if potentially dangerous, joy.

It's impossible to verify who invented the Martini – some claim it was Jerry Thomas, author of the seminal *Bar-Tender's Guide* of 1862, in San Francisco's Occidental Hotel for a miner from the town of Martinez in California who had struck gold and was in the mood to celebrate. Others say that it was a bartender named Martini di Arma di Taggia at New York's Knickerbocker Hotel in the early 20th century. Or was it just a shortening of a 'Martini and gin' – Martini & Rossi being a brand of Italian vermouth first produced in 1863? Whatever.

What we do know is that by the 1920s, the Martini had become the cocktail *du jour*, and its further associations with glamorous and celebrated drinkers – Dorothy Parker, Ernest Hemingway, F. Scott Fitzgerald, Marlene Dietrich, and Humphrey Bogart – ensured its popularity continued to grow.

In the days of prohibition in America, gin was distilled illegally and was notoriously foul of flavour. The addition of vermouth made it more palatable and the drink added up to something much more than the sum of its parts. The original recipe was likely to be something close to half and half (known as a wet Martini; the more vermouth you use, the 'wetter' it becomes), but as the quality of gin improved in the following decades, the fashion became for the drinks to become drier by holding back on the vermouth and upping the gin. This does, it should be noted, also make the drink more alcoholic. Martinis became even drier in the UK and America during WWII as exports of Italian and French vermouths dried up during Nazi occupation.

Noël Coward was another Martini lover, and he liked them very, very dry. His recipe was to 'fill a glass with gin and wave it in the general direction of Italy', while Winston Churchill's advice was to merely whisper the word 'vermouth' as you drank the gin. I'm also rather partial to Julia Child's 'reverse Martini' – a glass of Noilly Prat vermouth over ice with a splash of gin on top. Recommended for daytime drinking or when there's a need to err on the side of caution.

Most bartenders would agree that James Bond, another famous imbiber, was mistaken in his request for his Martini to be 'shaken not stirred' – shaking the ingredients makes the drink cloudy.

However you take your Martinis, I urge you to heed Dorothy Parker's dictum: I have put it to the test on more than one ill-judged occasion and can vouch for its good sense. 'I love to drink Martinis, but two at the very most. After three I'm under the table, after four I'm under the host.'

3

GIN AND IT

50ML/2OZ GIN
50ML/2OZ MARTINI ROSSO
GRIOTTE CHERRIES, TO GARNISH

Stir the gin and Martini over ice and strain into a chilled coupe.
Garnish with griotte cherries.

THE GIN AND IT – gin and Italian vermouth – is one of my favourite cocktails of all. It appears in many old movies and novels, but inexplicably seems to have fallen out of favour.

They were a favourite of the late and very great Dick Bradsell, the man credited with singlehandedly reviving the British cocktail scene in the 1980s and beyond, bringing to the bar proper, grown-up tinctures that continue to make our hearts beat that little bit faster. This is the man who gave the world the Bramble, the Treacle, the Pink Chihuahua and, perhaps most famously of all, the Espresso Martini. The latter was invented for a certain young super-model who asked him to make her 'something that will wake me up, then fuck me up'. Dick, the consummate pro, gave his customer just what she wanted.

In the 1950s, the Gin and It was probably two measures of gin to one of vermouth, served with ice in a tumbler, but this is Dick's version. It's a very versatile drink – try experimenting with different gins and vermouths in different proportions.

A Gin and It is essentially a Martini (though probably pre-dates it), but made with sweet (red) vermouth rather than the usual dry (white). I've dabbled with vermouth styles in between and can happily report that gin mixed with some of the richer white vermouths can make a very happy marriage, especially when garnished with a sprig of mint or perhaps some thyme. Stir over ice and strain if you wish, but this kind of drink also takes kindly to being knocked up in a tumbler on the rocks in a domestic setting.

4

GIMLET

50ML/2OZ GIN
35ML/1½OZ ROSE'S LIME JUICE CORDIAL

Serve in a tumbler over plenty of ice; no garnish required.

SCURVY WAS THE SCOURGE of sailors when European explorers sailed the seas in centuries past. A disease caused by lack of vitamin C, scurvy results in a slow and unpleasant death and it devastated crews on long voyages until, in the mid-18th century, it was discovered that citrus fruits helped keep scurvy at bay. Lemons and limes were carried on board, hence 'limey', the slang word for British seamen. In 1867, Lauchlin Rose, owner of a shipyard in Scotland, developed a recipe for lime juice preserved with sugar: Rose's Lime Juice Cordial was born and consequently saved the lives of countless seamen. Sailors mixed it with their daily rations of rum and water to make grog, while the officers preferred to mix it with neat gin.

In Raymond Chandler's 1954 novel *The Long Goodbye*, his hard-drinking private eye hero Philip Marlowe was a keen drinker of Gimlets, which were also Chandler's tipple of choice. 'Half gin and half Rose's Lime Cordial and nothing else,' is the recipe given in the book; he is quite specific that it should not contain fresh lime juice, as is now modish, though made in his way the drink is quite sweet for modern tastes, so I hold back on the cordial and up the gin. I think the fashion to use fresh lime juice in place of Rose's, somehow implying that it is morally superior, takes it into the realms of becoming a daiquiri and so rather defeats the point – a Gimlet is one of my store-cupboard cocktails, one that can be knocked up easily from ingredients I always have to hand. 'It beats Martinis hollow,' as the great detective said.

5

PINK GIN

6 DROPS OF ANGOSTURA BITTERS
50ML/2OZ GIN

*Slosh the Angostura bitters into a tumbler and swirl it around
so that it coats the sides. Add as much gin as you fancy.
Chuck in a couple of ice cubes and there you have it.*

WHOEVER DRINKS PINK GIN these days? Who even knows what it is?
Well, I do. It can lay claim to be one of the world's earliest cocktails, though
'cocktail' seems rather too fancy a word for a drink that is so simple.
Dating from around 1826 when HMS Hercules was patrolling the waters
of the Caribbean, the Pink Gin came about when the ship's surgeon
Henry Workshop came across Angostura bitters on one of his forays ashore.
Angostura contains antimalarial quinine but is far too bitter to be taken alone.
Captain Jack Bristol added it to his evening gin and discovered it was rare
good. He would probably have had no ice, but that doesn't mean you need to
go without.

6

BELLINI

AND VARIOUS FIZZY COUSINS

100ML/4OZ WHITE PEACH PURÉE
1 BOTTLE (70CL/25FL OZ) SPARKLING WINE

Stir the purée and wine together in a jug.
Pour slowly into chilled flutes, stirring gently as you go.

THE CLASSIC BELLINI, invented by Giuseppe Cipriani in 1948 at Venice's famous Harry's Bar and named after the 15th-century painter Giovanni Bellini, takes white peach purée and tops it up with prosecco.

Make your own purée by poaching very ripe peaches in a little water then straining through a fine sieve (sweeten it a little, if you like). Other summer fruits work well treated the same way – try raspberries, strawberries, black-currants or (my favourite) redcurrants. When autumn hits try blackberries, and in the depths of winter use rhubarb. Fruit liqueurs such as crème de cassis (blackcurrant), crème de mûre (blackberry) or even apricot brandy are a handy standby, and damson and sloe gin also work well.

Red vermouths rub along nicely with sparkling wine, and to my mind make brilliant aperitifs as their appetising bitterness broods in the background of the fruity bubbles. About 20ml/¾fl oz of vermouth in the bottom of a flute should do it, although the weight and intensity of your vermouth may mean you want to go lower or higher.

If I'm drinking decent fizz, it seems rather like gilding the lily to add any-thing else to its classy finesse. Sparkling wines of a more lowly pedigree, however, often respond well to a little gilding. Cheap fizz can be punishingly acidic after a glass or two, yet its edges can be so easily softened to give drinks real pizazz. Be aware that prosecco tends to have an underlying sweetness to it while cava is usually drier, so you may want to adjust things accordingly.

7

CAMPARI CORRETTO

25ML/1OZ CAMPARI
125ML/4¼OZ SPARKLING WINE
A FEW DROPS OF ORANGE BITTERS (OPTIONAL)

Pour the Campari into a flute and top up with sparkling wine.
The orange bitters are entirely optional but do transform
this drink into something rather sublime.

CAMPARI CORRETTO (meaning 'corrected') is a riff on the Bellini that uses Campari in place of the peach purée. I've selflessly tested this at some length and can report that it's best with a heavy hand on the Campari so that its personality stands out amid all the sparkles.

8

FRENCH 75

35—50ML/1½—2OZ LONDON DRY GIN
(DEPENDING ON HOW STRONG YOU'RE FEELING)
1 TBSP LEMON JUICE
1 TSP CASTER (SUPERFINE) SUGAR
(OR 1 TSP SUGAR SYRUP SHOULD YOU HAVE SOME TO HAND)
125ML/4¼OZ SPARKLING WINE
A TWIST OF LEMON

To make the drink properly, mix 'enough' dry gin with the lemon juice and sugar (or sugar syrup) in a cocktail shaker until the sugar has dissolved. Add a few cubes of ice and stir for 10 seconds then strain into a flute. Alternatively, just sling the gin, lemon juice and sugar into whatever glass you have to hand and give it a stir. Top up with sparkling wine and add a twist of lemon.

THIS DRINK HAS EVOLVED from the *Soixante-Quinze*, created in 1915 and named because it was so strong it feels like being shot with a French 75mm field gun, capable of firing 15 rounds per minute. Originally made with gin, apple brandy, grenadine and lemon juice, in 1926 Harry MacElhone, an American bartender in Paris, took a riff on it with gin, Calvados, grenadine and absinthe, and dubbed it the '75'.

Harry Craddock, in his 1930 *The Savoy Cocktail Book*, gives the recipe above (but serves it on the rocks) and calls it the 'French 75'. His one comment is: 'Hits with remarkable precision'. You have been warned.

9

'CHAMPAGNE' COCKTAIL

1 WHITE SUGAR CUBE
3–4 DROPS OF ANGOSTURA BITTERS
25ML/1OZ BRANDY
125ML/4¼OZ CHAMPAGNE
OR SPARKLING WINE

*Place the sugar cube in the base of a flute and add the
Angostura bitters and brandy. Top with well-chilled
fizz and away you go.*

IN A SIMILAR VEIN to the French 75, but with brandy in place of the gin, this drink is simpler and marginally less dangerous. I've no idea what Diana Dors drank, but for some reason this reminds me of her – a bit over the top and rather blousy, but jolly good fun at a party.

10

SPRITZ

**75ML/3OZ PROSECCO OR SPARKLING WINE
50ML/2OZ APEROL OR OTHER AMARO
25ML/1OZ (JUST A SPLASH) SODA
SLICE OF ORANGE OR LEMON, TO GARNISH**

*Combine the prosecco, Aperol and soda over ice in a large wine glass or
chunky tumbler. Garnish with a slice of lemon or orange.*

THE VENETIANS CAN arguably lay claim to have invented the spritz –
originally made with local amaro and white wine and lengthened with soda,
ideal to take the edge off the thirst at the end of a hot summer's day.

Aperol's masterful marketing brought the drink to the grateful masses in
the early 2000s and Aperol Spritz is now Venice's favourite aperitif. Their
easy-to-remember 3:2:1 prosecco:Aperol:soda recipe is a pretty good benchmark, although I encourage you to experiment with things other than Aperol:
Campari, of course, as well as Cynar (see page 53), but red vermouths with a
bit of oomph can work really well too – try Antica Formula or Punt e Mes.

The important thing is to retain the integrity of the base drink – too much
prosecco and/or soda will render your spritz weak and dreary. And the wine
needn't necessarily be prosecco – cava works just as well and is less sweet, or
use an un-fizzy, workaday white wine for something somewhat less spritzy but
still charming.

11

NEGRONI

1 PART CAMPARI
1 PART BEEFEATER GIN
1 PART MARTINI ROSSO
ORANGE PEEL, TO GARNISH

*Pour the Campari, gin and Martini over ice in a rocks glass or
tumbler and garnish with orange peel.*

NEEDING NO INTRODUCTION, the Negroni is not only one of the most delicious aperitifs, it's also one of the easiest to knock up, which perhaps goes some way to explaining its popularity. It is said to have been invented in Florence in 1919 when Count Camillo Negroni, home from a stint as a cowboy in America's Wild West where he'd developed a taste for hard liquor, ordered his bartender to make his favourite drink, the Americano (Campari, vermouth and a splash of soda water) with gin in place of the soda. Clever Count Negroni: his eponymous cocktail became one of the world's greatest, and still appears in the top 10 favourite aperitif lists of the drinkers I like and respect most of all.

The classic I was taught uses equal measures of Campari, Beefeater gin and Martini Rosso. Most bars use 25ml/1oz of each; that's a lot of booze packed into not many sips. Two Negronis as an aperitif are more than enough for me; after three the alcohol has killed off my appetite as well as my taste buds and I become a danger in the kitchen.

Using different gins and vermouths will obviously change the drink. Experiment with what you have to hand, but be cautious of going too off piste if you want the proper Negroni vibe. Steer away from floral gins as they battle a bit with the intrinsic bitterness of the drink; I find Antica Formula too sweet and heavy in the place of the Martini Rosso but it has its aficionados; I prefer Punt e Mes, swarthy with an extra kick of bitterness that makes the drink really intriguing. And while it's a drink that is hard to improve on, a dash of orange bitters can raise it to the ranks of the sublime.

12

NEGRONI SBAGLIATO

25ML/1OZ CAMPARI
25ML/1OZ RED VERMOUTH
125ML/4¼OZ SPARKLING WINE
ORANGE SLICE, TO GARNISH (OPTIONAL)

Pour the Campari and vermouth into a tumbler
or flute and top up with fizz.

THIS IS A RIFF on a Negroni, 'sbagliato' meaning 'incorrect'. It was supposedly invented by a barman in Bar Basso in Milan when he inadvertently reached for the prosecco and not the gin.

As with so many of these drinks, the vermouth you choose is up to you. Martini Rosso is the standard here but I rather like it with something a bit lighter – Regal Rogue's Bold Red vermouth really rocks my boat.

Some people serve Sbagliati in flutes but I prefer a tumbler with ice and a slice of orange, just as in a classic Negroni.

While we're on the subject of substitutions in classic Negronis, if you replace the gin with tequila you have a Jalisco Negroni; swap the gin for rum and it becomes a Kingston Negroni. And if you're feeling very brave, simply replace the Campari with a teaspoon (no more) of Fernet Branca and you have an approximation of a Hanky Panky, mentioned here as a nod to Ada Coleman, who invented it in around 1920 when she was head bartender at London's Savoy Hotel. Attagirl, Ada.

13

CARDINALE

1 PART CAMPARI
1 PART GIN
1 PART DRY WHITE VERMOUTH
LEMON PEEL, TO GARNISH

Pour the Campari, gin and vermouth over ice in a tumbler
and garnish with lemon peel.

PUT SIMPLY, this is a Negroni that substitutes the red vermouth with white. Recipes vary as to proportions; the classic 1:1:1 generally works for me, though it's worth experimenting depending on what gin and vermouth you're using. I'd stick to a London dry gin, probably Beefeater, but my choice of vermouth would depend on how I'm feeling and what I've got in my cocktail cupboard. Noilly Prat or Martini Extra Dry will lend the classic Cardinale vibe; something a bit richer such as Cocchi Americano bianco or Lustau's vermut blanco will add more opulence and depth.

14

BOULEVARDIER

1 PART CAMPARI
1 PART BOURBON
1 PART MARTINI ROSSO OR SIMILAR RED VERMOUTH
LEMON PEEL, TO GARNISH

Pour the Campari, whiskey and vermouth over ice in a rocks glass or tumbler and garnish with lemon peel.

THIS DRINK IS ATTRIBUTED to Erskine Gwynne, 'cherub-faced and rumpus-raising' scion of the Vanderbilt clan, once the richest family in America. Like many Americans partial to a tipple and with the means to afford a ticket, Erskine left prohibition-era New York and crossed the Atlantic to raise rumpuses in the drinking dens of Europe. He moved to Paris where he frittered away his share of the family's fortunes by publishing a magazine called *Boulevardier*, named after the French word for a man-about-town frequenting fashionable boulevards and their bars at his leisure. Ostensibly *Boulevardier* was a 'literary' journal but in fact was more of a gossipy society mag aimed at dissolute expat boulevardiers such as Erskine himself.

Erskine drank at fellow New Yorker Harry MacElhone's eponymous Harry's New York Bar where he rubbed elbows with predictable regulars such as F. Scott Fitzgerald, Ernest Hemingway, Noël Coward and James Joyce, all of whom had work that appeared in the magazine. In his 1927 book *Barflies and Cocktails* Harry credits Erskine as inventing this drink.

The Boulevardier is essentially a Negroni where the gin is replaced with bourbon whiskey, giving the drink a macho depth invoking wood and leather. The original was equal measures of each ingredient, and that's what I prefer, although more modern recipes often double up on the bourbon. I see no reason not to use other whiskeys if that's what you've got to hand; in fact I prefer mine made with a peaty whisky such as Laphroaig which is less sweet than most bourbons and brings a pleasing smokiness to the drink.

15

SUZE NEGRONI

25ML/1OZ GIN
25ML/1OZ WHITE VERMOUTH
OR SOMETHING A BIT FRUITY SUCH AS
LILLET BLANC OR COCCHI AMERICANO BIANCO
25ML/1OZ SUZE
WEDGE OF LIME OR BERGAMOT, TO SERVE

Build as per a normal Negroni, over ice in chunky tumbler. If you happen to have a bergamot to hand, a twist of its knobbly peel would only add to the drink's exotic appeal. Lime would work fine if you don't.

SUZE HAS A WONDERFUL fragrant, floral bitterness and here takes the place of Campari, while white vermouth is there instead of the red. Like all Negronis, this is pretty pokey if made to standard strength as above; if I'm feeling abstemious, I might make a smaller quantity, perhaps using the cap of a bottle as a measure (which holds about 10ml) mixed in a little glass, and that generally hits the spot. I might have another if it doesn't.

16

AMERICANO SHANDY

MAKES 2
25ML/1OZ CAMPARI
25ML/1OZ RED VERMOUTH
330ML/12OZ LAGER

Divide the Campari and vermouth between two glasses; the shape is up to you. Add ice and top up each glass with the lager, stirring gently to mix.

ARE YOU MAD? THEY SAID. Possibly, I replied, but let's try it anyway. Campari and sweet vermouth rub along surprisingly well here with hoppy lager to make a thirst-quenching shandy with a certain Italian élan. Most beers come in 330ml cans or bottles, just the right amount to make two drinks.

I'm proud to say that Elliot Lidstone and his partner Tessa put this drink on the menu at their much-lauded Box-E restaurant in Bristol. One could not wish for higher approbation for something that seemed a bit bonkers but really works well.

17

BICICLETTA

SPLASH OF CAMPARI
DRY WHITE WINE
SODA WATER (OPTIONAL)
LEMON SLICE, TO GARNISH

*Slosh the campari into a wine glass and top up with chilled white wine. Add
a splash of soda water if liked. Garnish with a slice of lemon.*

A GENEROUS SLUG of Campari with white wine in a wine glass and perhaps a splash of soda water: the Bicicletta is a classic and very easy Italian
aperitif with very good reason. Supposedly named in acknowledgement of the
gentlemen who'd weave home on their bicycles after one too many at their
local bar, it's a nifty way of covering the shame of a dreary pinot grigio or
other cheap white wine. Don't drown it out with too much soda; just make
sure the Campari and wine come straight from the fridge. Another store-
cupboard aperitif for which it's easy to develop a taste.

18

FINO AND FIZZ

50ML/2OZ FINO SHERRY
15ML/¹/₃OZ APRICOT LIQUEUR
SODA WATER
1 SPRIG BASIL AND 1 GREEN OLIVE, TO GARNISH

*Mix the sherry and liqueur in a large wine glass, add plenty
of ice and top with soda water. Give it a stir then garnish
with a sprig of basil and a green olive.*

SHAMELESSLY LIFTED from Ryan Chetiyawardana's book *Good Things
to Drink* (he calls his drink Bubbles and Byass), this shows how brilliantly dry
sherry can work in a long drink. Any cheap and cheerful fino will do, or try it
with amontillado for more nutty depth.

19

REBUJITO

75ML/3OZ MANZANILLA OR FINO SHERRY
ABOUT 150ML/6OZ LEMONADE
1 SPRIG FRESH MINT AND/OR
1 GREEN OLIVE, TO GARNISH

Serve in a tall glass over plenty of ice.

THIS CLASSIC ANDALUSIAN APERITIF uses manzanilla or fino sherry and is fantastic in the summer; use an amontillado or an oloroso instead for something a bit more profound but equally delicious and more fitting for winter. Spanish lemonade is somewhat less sweet than those the Brits and Americans are used to, so I'd top it with a splash of soda to cut the sweetness. I sometimes throw caution to the wind and use tonic water instead of lemonade.

20

WHITE PORT & TONIC

75ML/3OZ WHITE PORT
TONIC WATER
A SLICE OR WEDGE OF LEMON, TO GARNISH
A SPRIG OF ROSEMARY, TO GARNISH

Pour the white port into a tall glass over ice. Top up with tonic water, to taste, and garnish with the lemon and rosemary.

I TIP MY HAT to a band called the Four Deuces who recorded a song in 1956 called 'WPLJ' – white port and lemon juice – which was later covered by Frank Zappa. No recipe is given in the lyrics but I read it as a comfortable sufficiency of white port slugged over ice with a generous wedge of lemon to squeeze over it. As the chorus to the song so aptly puts it:

I feel so good
I feel so fine
I got plenty lovin'
And I got plenty wine.

Having said that, I treat white port in the same way as I do with most pale fortified wines: lovely chilled alone or over some ice, or sensationally delicious when mixed with tonic in this way. White port and tonic can handle all sorts of garnishes – I tinker happily with thyme, basil, mint or even cinnamon; but I love the rasping austerity of rosemary. Lemon is always my citrus of choice.

21

FIRST OF THE SUMMER WINE

50ML/2OZ GIN
20ML/³/₄OZ TAWNY PORT
2 TSP LEMON JUICE
TONIC WATER
MINT LEAVES, THYME AND ORANGE SLICES, TO GARNISH

Take a high-ball glass, or something similar, load it with ice and sling in the gin. Pour over the port and the lemon juice, give it a stir then top up with tonic. Go large on the garnish – some mint leaves, a sprig of thyme and a generous slice of orange.

THIS IS FROM ONE of my favourite bars in the world, Hausbar in Bristol, where German-born Aurelius Braunbarth brought Berlin basement bar chic to the fortunate few and has never been bettered, in Bristol at least. Gone but very much not forgotten, in 12 years of glorious rule Auri and his much-feted protégées at Hausbar made me so many perfect drinks I'd never attempt to recreate at home, such is the skill and attention to critical detail with which they were made. This one is easy to knock up at home; 'It's just a posh G&T,' says Auri, with characteristic cool. Choose whatever gin you like, bearing in mind you don't want to overpower the gorgeous, delicate fruitiness of the port.

22

VERMOUTHS ALONE IN ALL THEIR GLORY

MUCH AS I LOVE A NEGRONI or a good Martini, a Gin and It or a Cardinale, I really enjoy drinking vermouths alone, chilled from the fridge with maybe some ice and a slice of lemon, lime or orange. I learnt to drink vermouth this way in Barcelona almost a decade ago when an art historian I'd met in Gaudi's astonishingly bonkers Sagrada Família cathedral took me down an alley and introduced me to the Spanish way of drinking what they call vermuts. I was totally hooked and remain so to this day.

White or red, they charm me both, though the Spanish tend to favour the red. It's a drink to sip and enjoy at leisure: its bitterness really wakes up the taste buds and its intense botanicals always intrigue. Orange is the most usual garnish in Spain, along with a fat green olive on a stick whose salty notes give a dashing finish to the drink. Lemon or lime often suit dry vermouths better but there are really no rules to follow. Consider the characteristics of your chosen vermouth/vermut and pick something you think might suit.

23

MANHATTAN

**2 PARTS RYE WHISKEY
1 PART RED VERMOUTH
A FEW DASHES OF ANGOSTURA BITTERS
MARASCHINO CHERRY, TO GARNISH**

Stir together the whiskey and vermouth in a tumbler or cocktail shaker over ice, and add a few dashes of Angostura bitters. Strain into a chilled cocktail glass, garnished with a maraschino cherry.

A MANHATTAN APPEARS here because it is one of *the* classic vermouth cocktails, though it's one I rarely make at home; I prefer to drink it in a darkened bar with the promise of a debauched night ahead. Very *Mad Men*.

24

ALBA ROSSA

25ML/1OZ ROSÉ VERMOUTH
75ML/3OZ PINK GRAPEFRUIT JUICE
SODA WATER
FEW DROPS GRAPEFRUIT BITTERS (OPTIONAL)

Stir together the vermouth and grapefruit juice over ice in whatever glass you think might suit. Top up with soda water and add grapefruit bitters to taste, if liked.

ROSÉ VERMOUTHS are a fairly new innovation, combining the red-berry fruitiness of their red cousins with the freshness of their white ones. Try Regal Rogue Wild Rose, Belsazar Rosé or Cocchi Rosa in this. I'm not a massive fan of fruit juices in aperitifs but here pink grapefruit adds its own pleasing bitterness and the soda stops it being too sticky.

25

MAURESQUE

35ML/1½OZ PASTIS
25ML/1OZ ORGEAT
ABOUT 100ML/4OZ CHILLED WATER

Pour the pastis and orgeat into a tall glass and pour over the chilled water.
Add ice cubes – adjust to taste with more water if liked,
et Robert est votre oncle.

A PASTIS SERVED in the classical way hits the spot for me almost every time, but if I do feel like a change and pretend I'm in a bar in the south of France, I might knock up a Mauresque.

The French are fond of their syrups and make them from almost anything that grows. They mix them with water to give to children and use them in drinks for grown-ups too. Orgeat is almond syrup and when mixed with pastis makes a very *ooh-la-la* sharpener for those with a penchant for anise.

If you replace the orgeat with grenadine (pomegranate syrup) you have a Tomate; strawberry syrup makes a pretty Rourou, while if you use crème de menthe you get a bright-green Perroquet.

26

DEATH IN THE AFTERNOON

25ML/1OZ ABSINTHE
125ML/4¾OZ CHAMPAGNE OR SPARKLING WINE

Pour the absinthe into a flute and top up with the
champagne or sparkling wine.
Pray to the Lord for mercy.

THIS DELIRIOUSLY DECADENT drink was allegedly invented by Ernest Hemingway, which pretty much tells you all you need to know. Champagne and absinthe? What could possibly go wrong?

27

WHISKEY SODA

ABOUT 50ML/2OZ WHISKEY
ABOUT 200ML/7OZ SODA WATER

Pour the whiskey into a tumbler (see below),
then add the soda water.

I **HAVE PURPOSEFULLY** avoided any mention of brown spirits in this book, partly for reasons of space but mostly because, for me, they don't really fit into my frame of aperitif reference points, though I know there are many who would disagree. But I can quite see the appeal of a large bourbon on the rocks at the end of a heavy day, and of course a Mojito made well with good rum is a joyous thing if the day has also been hot, so please forgive any perceived oversight.

I will give one recipe, however, if you can call it that. The Whiskey Soda was my grandfather's noggin (my grandmother preferred 'just a tiny sherry') and it holds a place in my heart for this reason. Also, it does make a very good and easy aperitif, one of the simplest and most soothing there is. I spell it with an 'e' because my grandfather was Irish and Jameson was what he drank – only whiskies made in Scotland (or Japan) may be spelled 'whisky'. Choose whatever style of whiskey you like but this bashful drink doesn't demand any-thing special. For me it's something to drink alone and contemplatively, quite possibly before and/or after a fish finger sandwich supper.

My grandfather always used a heavy, cut-glass tumbler, but anything that feels nice in your hand will do; choose a size to suit your thirst then add a couple of fingers of whiskey and four, no more, of soda water, ideally from an old-fashioned soda syphon. That's it. No ice.

28

BAR TERMINI'S MARSALA MARTINI

50ML/2OZ GIN
(BAR TERMINI USES BEEFEATER)
12.5ML/½OZ DRY MARSALA
½TSP DRY VERMOUTH
(MARTINI EXTRA DRY IS MY PREFERENCE)
1 DASH ORANGE BITTERS
(BAR TERMINI MAKES ITS OWN ALMOND BITTERS)

TO MAKE THE PICKLED ALMONDS:
12 SKINNED, BLANCHED ALMONDS
ABOUT 150ML/5OZ CIDER VINEGAR
1 TSP SALT

*For the pickled almonds, put the almonds in a small jar or bowl.
Cover with champagne or cider vinegar, stir in the salt gently until it has
dissolved, then leave covered for 24 hours. Drain off the liquid and
set the almonds aside (they will keep for 2 weeks in an airtight tin).*

*Stir the ingredients over plenty of ice just enough to chill them – ten stirs
should do it. Strain into a beautiful glass, drop in a pickled almond, stand
back and watch your guests swoon. Mamma mia.*

TONY CONIGLIARO is a shining star in the London cocktail firmament whose killer drinks have been making serious drinkers go weak at the knees for years. He is the brains behind Bar Termini, a tiny bar on Old Compton Street in Soho modelled on the bar at the train station in Rome (and he now has a branch in Marylebone). This is my favourite of his many splendid drinks. The pickled almond is essential to the drink: a jewel to be scraped out of the bottom of the glass with your finger and eaten with the final swig of this very clever aperitif, so you do need to plan ahead, but only by 24 hours or thereabouts.

29

ADONIS

15G/½OZ COFFEE BEANS,
PLUS A FEW EXTRA, TO GARNISH
250ML/10OZ SWEET VERMOUTH
(I LIKE MARTINI RISERVA SPECIALE RUBINO)
250ML/10OZ FINO SHERRY
(IT ALSO WORKS WITH AMONTILLADO)
1 TSP ORANGE BITTERS

Add the coffee beans to the vermouth, let them infuse at room temperature
for about 15 minutes, then strain. Mix the vermouth with the sherry and
pour into a clean bottle. Chill well, finishing it off in the freezer if you're in
a hurry, then serve in small chilled glasses. Garnish with a coffee bean or
three (odd numbers always seem to look more pleasing than even) if you like.
This quantity makes 10 servings and will keep in a fridge for two weeks.

ALLEGEDLY INVENTED IN NEW YORK in 1884 in honour of the Broadway musical of the same name, the Adonis is a great mash up of two of my favourite things – sherry and vermouth. Some recipes call for more sherry than vermouth but I prefer equal measures. The coffee beans are not in the original recipe but are a clever addition given to me by drinks writer Richard Godwin; they give the drink a lovely depth but are a bit of a faff if you're only making a couple of drinks which is why I tend to make up a batch using the above recipe and keep the bottle in the door of my fridge.

If you don't use the coffee beans, it's still a killer drink. Chill the vermouth and the sherry before you mix it, or quickly stir them over ice and strain into the glasses. A good 25ml/1oz each of sherry and vermouth makes a nice nip, but feel free to use more if you're in the mood for a stronger hit.

30

BAMBOO

1 PART DRY VERMOUTH
1 PART AMONTILLADO SHERRY
ORANGE BITTERS

Mix up as an individual drink on the rocks, or stirred over ice if you can be bothered. Alternatively, mix up a batch in advance. Half a bottle each of vermouth and sherry and a teaspoon or thereabouts of orange bitters, mixed in a bottle and kept in the fridge to be served when and however you fancy it.

'**ONE OF THE LATEST** and most insidious drinks was recently introduced into swell saloons in this city by an Englishman. Consists of three parts sherry and one part vermouth. It is called "Bamboo" probably because after imbibing it the drinker feels like "raising Cain".' So the *St Paul Daily Globe* sanctimoniously pronounced in Minnesota in 1886, in one of the earliest references to this drink which mixes sherry and vermouth with such aplomb.

Recipes vary wildly: the sherry is sometimes fino, sometimes amontillado or occasionally a costly palo cortado, while both sweet and dry vermouths appear, sometimes both together. Here I take my lead from Felix Cohen at his wonderful bar Every Cloud in London, whose taste I trust implicitly. Felix favours Martini Extra Dry or Lillet Blanc as the vermouth, while Harvey's amontillado is his sherry of choice.

31

ROSE PETAL VODKA

MAKES 1 BOTTLE
6 HEAVILY SCENTED ROSES IN THE PRIME
OF BLOOM, FRESHLY PICKED
1 BOTTLE (70CL/25FL OZ) VODKA

*Remove the petals from three roses, place in a glass or plastic container and
pour over the vodka. Leave to infuse for 4 or 5 days, then remove the petals
(the colour will have disappeared). Pick three more roses and add their petals
to the vodka, leave for 4 more days then strain and transfer to a clean bottle.*

ROSE PETAL VODKA captures an English country garden in the summer and
I'm indebted to food writer Felicity Cloake for this recipe from her lovely book
The A–Z of Eating. Use the vodka to make a Martini with a gently flavoured
vermouth – Belsazar Rosé makes a very charming pairing – or sip it alone
very cold.

I frequently flavour vodkas, to drink alone or to use in cocktails. The process
is very simple: add whatever you like to vodka, leave it to macerate for a few
days then strain and put it into a bottle. Citrus peel and summer berries work
particularly well, as do spices and woody herbs, perhaps used in conjunction
with each other, sweetened or not according to your taste. Chilli vodka – slice
a couple of red chillies vertically – gives an invigorating kick to a bloody Mary.
Some people use sweets (candy) such as jelly beans or gummy bears; I would
rather die.

Marmalade vodka is very fitting for winter. Take a jar of good marmalade,
ideally homemade, and heat it gently in a small pan until it liquefies. Stir in
a bottle of vodka, transfer to a jar or plastic tub and leave for a week or so,
stirring or shaking it from time to time, then strain it through a fine sieve and
then a muslin cloth and transfer to a clean bottle. Drink it by itself, chilled or
not, when you want a warming lift; it also makes a brilliant Negroni when
used in place of the gin and with the addition of a dash of orange bitters.

32

GREEN WALNUT RIKIKI

MAKES 2 LITRES/3½ PINTS
8 GREEN WALNUTS, PICKED ON OR JUST BEFORE 14 JULY
500ML/18OZ EAU DE VIE
1.5 LITRES/2 PINTS 14FL OZ RED WINE
500G/1LB 2OZ SUGAR

Pierce each walnut through the middle with a knitting needle – it should go easily through the nut's skin without any resistance. Place in a large plastic container then pour over the eau de vie, ensuring the nuts are covered. Cover and leave for 3 weeks.

In a large saucepan, heat the red wine gently and add the sugar. Stir until the sugar has dissolved. Add the red wine syrup to the walnuts, cover and leave for 3 months. Drink over ice or as a warming tot on Bonfire Night or Thanksgiving.

YOU WON'T FIND RIKIKI on any internet search, or in any dictionary of booze; it seems it is particular to a little sleepy corner of the Dordogne/ Charentes borders in France and refers to a drink made at home using local wine and eau de vie infused with nuts or fruit. The word may well be related to the Provençale verb *requinquilhar*, meaning to strengthen or to cheer up. It may also have something to do with the Spanish word *riquisimo*, meaning 'delicious', but then again it may not.

This recipe was given to me by an antiques dealer I met in a bar who carried a bottle of it around in his soft leather satchel. The recipe was given to him by his grandmother, who in turn inherited it from hers; it has rightfully stood the test of time. It's a slow burner – nearly four months from start to finish – but it's definitely worth the wait. It's dark as the devil with a captivating bittersweet warmth; make up a batch and sip it to lift the gloom of long winter nights.

33

VIN D'ORANGE

MAKES 1.5 LITRES
1 LARGE ORANGE, GENTLY WASHED
20 CLOVES
1 LITRE/35OZ UNFLAVOURED EAU DE VIE
500ML/18FL OZ SUGAR SYRUP
(MADE BY DISSOLVING 500G/18OZ SUGAR
IN 500ML/18FL OZ OF WARM WATER)

Stud the orange all over with the cloves, then put it in a glass or plastic bowl. Pour over the eau de vie. Cover and leave to infuse for 2 weeks. Transfer to a larger vessel and add the sugar syrup. Cover and set aside for a whole 2 months. Strain, chill, then drink. Très chic.

THIS IS A REALLY RANDOM recipe, given to me by a Frenchman who's better off forgotten. It's very simple but needs patience, much like the Frenchman himself, as it takes a couple of months from start to finish. It's a lovely thing to have in your fridge – it'll last for months – either to drink on its own or to fiddle around with; it adds a certain flair to cheap fizz that needs perking up and is also really, really good mixed with Campari or something similar on the rocks with a splash of soda.

INDEX

ACKNOWLEDGEMENTS

Massive thanks to Sarah Lavelle at Quadrille for putting the idea of this book in my head to start with, to Harriet Webster for holding my hand as we went to the wire, and to Will Webb, Sarah Hogan and Alexander Breeze who designed, photographed and styled *Aperitif* into a thing of such beauty.

Aurelias Braunbarth of the late and very much lamented Hausbar for words of wisdom, drinks of perfection and more than a decade of superlative hospitality; Felix Cohen of the wonderful Every Cloud bar for A-class geekery and sometimes-mad-but-always-knockout libations; Tony Conigliaro and Robin Kolek at Bar Termini, Jack Bevan, Dick Bradsell (RIP), Lionel Carrère, Ryan Chetiyawardana (aka Mr Lyan), Felicity Cloake, Richard Godwin, Ian Kellett, Harry Martini, Mark Ward and Andrew Wiggins for sharing recipes and/or secrets.

The many who have shared their excellent palates and good company along my long and arduous journey, including Fiona Beckett, Tom Harvey, Martin Lam, Louise Marchionne, Timantha Romain, Jane Selman, Raj Soni, Philip Sweeney, John Stokes, Claire Thomson, Matt Williamson, Jonathan Woods and all the staff at Bellita and Bell's Diner. Special thanks to Barny Haughton for the above, as well as introducing me to the Madeira Club and reintroducing me to Campari Soda 25 years ago, and to Mike Smith for endlessly enthusiastic tasting above and beyond a lodger's call of duty, rock star gossip and for hitting on the wheeze of the Marmalade Negroni.

Bob Granleese, Chris Losh and Laura Rowe for regularly paying me to write bollocks about booze for their various organs; Tim Hayward for providing Scrivener, a sports car and succour from start to finish; and Shawn Hennessey, Tim Holt, Lionel Lamadon, Sue Miller, Russell Norman, Arne Ringner and Christine Smallwood for insider info on places they know better than I.

Thanks also to Sof and Hank Terry, and Bridget and Richard Sudworth, for providing sanctuary in their idyllic necks of various woods, Deirdre and Phil Hardwick for eggs and herbal medicine when I needed them most, Emma and Joe Wadsack for the fan and imperative sherry know-how, Peter Ross at Guildhall Library for access to his incredible annals, and Peter Barham from Bristol University for putting me straight on rockhopper penguins and other scientific matters.

And finally, thanks to my family, those dead and alive. My parents and grandparents, who brought me up to understand what noggins are all about, my wonderful siblings and their offspring who continue to fly that flag with such alacrity, and to Binks, my daughter, who is my harshest critic but my proudest achievement.